BEYOND OUR GHETTOS

Gay Theology in Ecological Perspective

J. MICHAEL CLARK

Beyond Our Ghettos

Beyond Our Ghettos

Gay Theology in Ecological Perspective

▼

J. Michael Clark

The Pilgrim Press
Cleveland, Ohio

The Pilgrim Press, Cleveland, Ohio 44115
© 1993 by J. Michael Clark

Library of Congress Cataloging-in-Publication Data

Clark, J. Michael (John Michael), 1953–
Beyond our ghettos : gay theology in ecological perspective /
J. Michael Clark.
p.   cm.
Includes bibliographical references and index.
ISBN 0-8298-0959-7
1. Homosexuality—Religious aspects.   2. Human ecology—Religious
aspects.   I. Title.
BL65.H64C58   1993
291.1'7835766—dc20   93-4196
CIP

For these heroes all . . .
that ever-growing list of friends and acquaintances
who have gone from us during the years
in which AIDS has plundered our community,
friends whom we will always cherish and remember—

Wayne Abernathy
Ed Acree
Bill Adams
Ray Alfond
Jim Bennett
Serge Bernstein
Claude Branque
Glenn Breslin
Jason Byars
Corky Chandler
Ed Coalter
"Ralph" Delgado
Michael Dollins
Jaye Evans
Jim Flach
Gus Galvez
Roger Gardner
Neil Gregory
Judd Herndon
Lee Hopper

John Howell
John Huber
John Klein
Ray Kluka
Bill K. Lane
Bill Lang
Greg Lewis
Buddy Lueth
Jon Martin
Max Meltzer
Jimmie Miles
Chris Minor
Robbie Moore
Ronnie Moore
Robert Needle
David O'Shields
Gary Piccola
Don Pletzke
Jerry Pyszka
Tim Ragan

Steve Robards
Tom Roeder
Melvin Ross
John Routh
Dennis Rudd
Fred Seal
Randy Sink
Charlie St. John
Michael Stark
Errol Statum
Don Stogner
Tom Tester
Ricky Turner
Kerry Vanderwall
Doug Vines
Raz Walker
Johnny Walsh
Mark Waters
Robert West II
Mark Wood

—may their energies remain alive with us,
informing our every effort toward liberation.

"The hero is commonly the simplest and obscurest of men."

—Henry David Thoreau, "Walking"

Contents

▼

Preface:
An Eclectic Ecology and Religion
▼

Doing theology is an activity that can take many forms—biblical theology, patristic theology, historical theology, systematic theology, process theology, and liberation theology, to cite but some possibilities. Although the phrase "liberation theology," as such, is most often associated with Latin American liberation theology, the theological activity of other minority groups—African Americans, women, and gay men and lesbians—belongs to this same tradition. The bulk of gay liberation theology is also an *eclectic* activity, if you will, using the paradigms and analyses of other writers as starting points. By bringing these paradigms (thesis) into dialogue with gay and lesbian experience (antithesis), a new liberational synthesis emerges. The most frequently used paradigms for shaping the activity of gay liberation theology have been those of feminist theology, as we compare the structures of sexism and heterosexism, although Latin American paradigms have also been used.[1] Apart from these creative extensions of other paradigms, gay theology has also been pursued in the existential or phenomenological manner, beginning with our experience *first*, particularly insofar as that has been shaped by AIDS.[2]

My own contributions to gay theology and ethics also fall within the eclectic style, not only drawing upon primarily feminist and process theologies, but also ranging widely over gay male experience in mythology, history, and literature, as well as drawing upon our collective lived experience since Stonewall; I have also included my own idiosyncratic autobiographical experience and family history within the full scope of my theological resources.[3] Throughout this progression of reflective activity, my primary standpoint for perceiving, thinking, writing, and speaking publicly has been my existential location as a particular gay man within the primarily gay male subculture.

Consequently, while over the last several years I have come to realize and to appreciate the fact that the activity of gay liberation theologizing is not and certainly should not be restricted to the gay/lesbian communities (it will not resonate with all gay people, while its breadth and connections with other liberation theologies will connect with many nongay people), I have also wondered to what extent it may nonetheless be a ghettoized activity. I have begun to question my own ghettoization as well. Particularly as I have lately become a curmudgeon on behalf of my community and have looked closely at the impact of masculine socialization on our gay male sexuality and our most intimate relationships, I have also begun to reevaluate the implications of the so-called urban gay ghetto.[4] While the urban ghettos or subcultures provide a welcome haven in which we are free to be ourselves, they can also restrict our vision and our participation in the larger world. They certainly have not protected us from homophobic antigay violence or from AIDS. At one particular point in my frustration with the psychosocial myopia of gay men—including myself at times—I quipped, "We also need to be at the forefront of ecological concerns to be healing the earth itself. As I get frustrated with people—and even with my gay and lesbian siblings whose cause I relentlessly champion even as I criticize us/me—I sometimes wonder if a nature given the respect it deserves is not far more trustworthy than people."[5]

The gauntlet had been thrown, the challenge declared; I was prophetically ensnared by my own words. Subsequently encouraged by the director of the Hughes Programs in Biology of Emory University, I took up the challenge, bringing my own eclectic style of theologizing to ecology, to the synthesis of ecology and religion. This book is the result of that engagement. If my closet door was irrevocably opened years ago, my immersion in ecological theory has now opened the gates of the ghetto for me as well, and I have been brought to a much more inclusive perspective for my activities of theology and praxis. I have found, for example, that my gay perspective can help extend the analyses of others and thereby create something new, something more liberating and healing. I can see how our experiences of homophobia, exclusion, and expendability in our society are also reflected in the ways our society disvalues and disposes of the earth itself. And my engagement with ecology has not only reshaped my own patterns of thinking and behaving; it has also, from the broader global perspective outside the ghetto's gates, empowered me to become even more militant in my advocacy for gay and lesbian people. I have, however, also come to see more clearly the extent to which such advocacy must also include all oppressed peoples and the earth itself. Now, in sharing with others my thoughts on these issues in detail, I hope that our ensuing dialogue will facilitate god/ess with us . . . and with all the earth.

To facilitate that dialogue, I want to invite the reader into an "ecology of language." Although I am no longer thin, I am a fairly small man—my mother never convinced me that five foot six was average and trying to find a size seven men's shoe will always be a challenge. Like my physical embodiment, my writing is usually tersely packed. Among the many professional hats I wear is that of part-time instructor of freshman English at Georgia State University. In my course on research writing, I encourage my students to develop that same terseness of style. Having to write twenty- to twenty-five-page term papers has not only been the bane of many a student's existence, it also encourages the excess verbiage of unnecessary padding. My students begin by writing half-page summaries or abstracts of published essays and eventually produce a five- to seven-page research paper or "documented essay." They learn that the same research and writing skills serve the small paper as well as the dissertation or booklength effort. In short, both my students and I develop an ecology of language where every word must count and where nothing is wasted.

This same economy of language has shaped the best recent liberation theology. The full host of feminist writers, for example, has realized that much of our everyday language is frequently sexist or otherwise inadequate for developing theologically sound discourse. Feminist theologians often create hyphenated word constructions to circumvent such dilemmas, and my own theological writing has been heavily influenced by both the content and style of their writing. Some examples may serve to illustrate: One of the simplest constructions serves to resolve any sexism in talk about the divine. Just as "he/she" and "s/he" are constructions that make English pronouns nonsexist, so the term "god/ess" works for the divine. To speak of "god/ess" is to suggest not only that the divine is both male and female in gender, but also that the divine is "pangendered" and "pansexual," embracing but not limited to all possible gender expressions and all possible sexual orientations. Another good example is that of "patriarchy," "heteropatriarchy," and their derivatives (e.g., heteropatriarchal). Again, the canon of feminist theology has described "patriarchy" as the system and structures of male privilege that are interwoven with Western society and culture. Gay theology argues that male privilege specifically defined as both not feminine and *not homosexual* is the real determinant of Western culture and theology. To reflect that difference, "heteropatriarchy" evokes the idea of straight male privilege.

With these brief comments and examples, I invite readers to explore and determine for themselves if good things come in small packages, if whether a small, terse book can in fact open up larger visions of how we might best heal the earth—and ourselves in the process. Our explorations of extant ecological theory, our reexaminations of theological concepts, and our occasional, playful reconstruction of language can encourage us along an inclusive and liberational pilgrimage. In the spirit of best facilitating that process, I must thank my editor at Pilgrim Press, Richard Brown, for his patience and diligence with me, helping me better to discern when terse, compact language is creative and when it is not. He has enabled me to hear another lesson I offer my students—that not only is spare, concise writing good writing, but also that, whenever possible, everyday language is clearer than jargon. Without Richard's help, this book in its published form would never have been possible. I am also deeply indebted to my spouse, Bob McNeir, and to Pat Marsteller of Emory University's Hughes Programs in Biology for their enthusiastic support while I have undertaken the research and writing of this book. Finally, a word of thanks must also be offered to you, the reader, for investing the time and commitment to share in dialogue and reflection. Together we can move beyond our various ghettoizations and take up the tasks of liberation, of embodying god/ess with us, for the sake of all the earth. Thank you.

Acknowledgments

▼

The author extends his deep appreciation for the time and space provided, in support of the research and writing of the present volume, by the Hughes Programs in Biology of Emory University, Patricia A. Marsteller, Ph.D., director.

The Emerald City
and What We Found There

"If people were Superior to Animals, they'd take better care of the world," said Pooh.

"That's true," I said.

But down through the centuries, man has developed a mind that separates him from the world of reality, the world of [nature].
—Benjamin Hoff, *The Tao of Pooh*

Confronting Our Ghettos, Healing Our Vision

When the rainbow shattered on a balmy night in June 1969, we stormed the gates of the Emerald City to demand both the end of harassment and discrimination and the acceptance and liberation of ourselves as gay and lesbian people. If that riot at the Stonewall Inn seemed to open a door into freedom, no longer walling us out, over the decades since we have unwittingly allowed ourselves to be walled within. Gaining access to the emerald cities that promised urban refuge from the lions and tigers and bears of our frequently rural and religious upbringings and from the goblins of our often homophobic families, small towns, and suburbs enabled us to gather together in lavender ghettos whose psychological confines just as often disempowered us even as they enabled us to be ourselves. As we exchanged our closets for our ghettos, new sexual freedoms and political battles intermingled, conflicted, and conjoined; we rode in celebration upon bright horses of different colors down yellow brick roads of our own creation, toward uncertain goals.[1]

In the midst of our urban celebrations, we found, however, that these new roads led not only to political and personal inroads, but to a deeper, denser forest filled with new ogres to block our path. Hearts of darkness imperiled the centers of our rainbow dreams: Anita Bryant, Jesse Helms, William Dannemeyer, and others brandished their particular fire and brimstone. AIDS assailed us, cyclone-like, sweeping far too many of us prematurely off the road forever. Safety in ghettoized numbers had not freed us from these phantasms;[2] the myopic vision of the ghetto's crystal ball had not prepared us for the antigay/lesbian violence or the AIDS-grief that have constituted our reality as we moved through the 1980s and into the 1990s. And so, we have come to realize that just as we assaulted the stone walls of oppression over two decades ago, we must now dismantle the invisible walls of our own making to create ever new visions of liberation and healing, while at the same time redoubling our assault upon the walls of exclusion, homophobia, and AIDS that still block our path and endanger our journey. Like those who have suffered oppression in all ages, we must work toward the day when all such dehumanizing walls come tumbling down.

One way to begin is to discern in passing the great multitude of psychological ghettos, all of which equally distort human vision and delimit worlds too restrictively small to enable liberation. *Religious ghettos* narrowly focus on denominational distinctions or scriptural inerrancy that exclude gay people from pulpit and redeemed and that turn outward only in defensive and self-righteous pronouncements upon, and actions against, those persons deemed unworthy of their too narrow love. *Academic ghettos* define the scope of so-called legitimate scholarship and craft a putative objectivity that brackets any creative diversity of methodologies and subjects into categories of "alternative life-styles" and thereby protects heterosexist literary criticism, religious studies, sociology, and other disciplines from intellectual "contamination." *Consumerist ghettos* sustain patriarchal values of growth economics and the Genesis ghetto mentality of dominion-over; consumerism creates myths of gay disposable income, forever trivializing gay men as ritzy materialists and lesbians as beansprout-laden, earthy nonconformists. *First-world ghettos* champion the white, upwardly mobile Westerner, while ignoring the needs of people of color and thereby creating so-called third worlds in our own cities as well as abroad. All of these ghettos of putative privilege function together to turn our earth into one large ghetto—exploited and exhausted—a nature as imperiled as our own gay and lesbian lives.

This ubiquity of ghetto mentalities, in collusion with the failure of our own ghettoization to save us from homophobia and AIDS, demands a broader vision. Gay liberation theology must also move beyond any narrow, latent myopia and thus also "break out of the conceptual trap"[3] of our ghettoization, at once realizing our oppression and marginality, our exclusion and disvaluation, while not becoming so preoccupied with our experience as gay people to the extent that we also create us-versus-them dichotomies. So-called gay theology must realize that it is not just for gay people. Some gay men and lesbians may feel no personal resonance with even a radical post-Judeo-Christian gay theologizing, while at the same time the analyses, theories, and visions generated out of gay/lesbian writers' experiences as gay people—as to the nature of god/ess' utter horizontality or immanence with us, as to human responsibility and our fundamental relationality and interdependence, as to the absolute value of justice as right-relation for all the earth—these visions will be shared in common with other liberation theologies and will belong to that ongoing tradition. For example, the demands of relational justice and responsibility in gay theology also imply the demand of *ecological* justice and responsibility: as gay men and lesbians, our deep existential understanding of exclusion and disvaluation, our liberational efforts, and our erotically empowered and loving relational embrace must be extended to all other oppressed persons (vs. sexism, racism, classism, etc.), to all persons generally (including, albeit difficult, loving those who oppress), and most certainly to all the earth as our equally valued and valuable copartner against all the forces of oppression, devaluation, disvaluation, exclusion, and exploitation that are arrayed against us. We cannot champion—in our theology or in our lives—the liberation of ourselves alone.

And yet, I realize that opening up gay theology in such fashion may not be easily acceptable. Some gay men and lesbians may balk at moving too quickly away from such in-house concerns as anti-gay/lesbian violence and AIDS. Many ecologists, already disturbed by their confrontation with ecofeminism, may homophobically shun any specifically gay/lesbian voice intruding upon "their" area of expertise. Consequently, I realize that, as Anne Primavesi has noted, "those who challenge or dismantle conceptual traps do so at their peril."[4] Such risk, however, is already part and parcel of even doing specifically gay/lesbian theology. Earlier, Judith Plaskow and Carol Christ acknowledged that "to choose to violate standards of scholarly objectivity by writing in a way that speaks to the whole self rather than the head is to run the often costly risks of scholarly depreciation or academic dismissal."[5] But if staying safely within the confines of either the academically acceptable or the gay/lesbian politically correct only furthers ghettoization and too narrow vision, the risk of offending these myopic standards must be assumed by the gay liberation theologian. Our liberation as gay and lesbian people cannot be achieved and will not occur in isolation from the needs of other oppressed persons or from the aching of our exploited earth. Our liberation requires a broader, ecological perspective, and bringing our theology and ecology into dialogue is an important first step for such an all-encompassing liberational effort.

In beginning to dismantle conceptual traps while bringing my own subjectivity and scholarship together, I must ask myself, can I begin to frame a theology from my encounter with ecology, and especially ecofeminism, which really is broad enough not only to en-compass and extend my previous work but also to help liberate all of us from ghettoization and ghettoized myopia? My gay ecological theology (or ecotheology) must insist that no ecological analysis or analytical paradigm goes far enough as long as gay men and lesbians or anyone or anything else remains invisible. We must insist that heteropatriarchal hierarchies and dualisms—cultural mindsets or "conceptual traps"—that not only devalue to exploit but disvalue to make certain people and the earth and any of its species dispo-sable—value*less*—must be utterly dismantled and justice as right-relation established in their stead. The demand of justice as caring right-relation applies to biosphere and geosphere as well as to hu-man beings. Liberation theology will abide no double standards; our healed vision must be broad enough to include "the earth and all that dwell therein."

REESTABLISHING A SENSE OF PLACE, REVALUING OUR HOMES

Other questions then emerge for me in the specificity of my partic-ular life as one particular gay male theologian: how does my mar-ginality, not only to the nongay world, academia, and religious institutions but to much of the mainstream gay male subculture as well, affect my theology and my values? If I have become somewhat reclusive in recent years, for example, can that have a positive value for my theologizing? How do reclusiveness and ecological perspective fit together? If I am a gay male and yet one not social-ized in a typically masculine fashion, one who is no longer willing to participate in the patriarchal politicking inherent in most groups and one who does not need any organizational identification for self-authentication, can I act and be iconoclastic on behalf of liber-ation as an individual and in my coupled commitment?[6] Or is this merely a smoke screen for a patriarchal ego-isolation opposed to community? I seem to find workable, genuine community limited to my spouse and myself and our interactions with a small handful of people, a few at a time, as around the table sharing a meal. Any larger group ends up feeling dysfunctional for me. Is that because groups, even proliberation, gay/lesbian groups always fall back unwittingly into patriarchal dynamics? Or is it simply because, like ecofeminist Judith Plant, I have begun to revalue my sense of place, to revalue the importance of home, realizing that the "*real work* is at home" and that home "is the theatre of our human ecology?"[7]

Surprisingly perhaps for a gay man, I want to reclaim and revalue the concepts of "home" and of "being at home"; I would even like, in a totally gender role-free way, to reclaim and revalue the term "homemaker" as well. Bob's and my home and all it entails (house, yard, garden, flowers and veggies, dogs, fish, friends, dinner guests, etc.) is where I am most comfortable right now. We see ourselves revaluing the interactions and activities of our home against the much-voiced demand that we be patrons at gay bars and members of gay groups, groups whose time requirements and lack of commitment to gay couples compete with our home and our relational priorities, people who are saying that doing the work of being a genuinely committed gay male couple in these times is not enough or is not good enough. In contrast, we believe there is intrinsic value in our mutual relationship without gender roles, as well as in our being at home in relation to each other and in relation to our particular microcosmic biosphere within our macrocosmic home, the earth.

I am gratified to discover that several ecofeminists also support such a valuational choice. Judith Plant, for example, has articulated the dilemma whereby the values and skills of life-giving, nurturing, meeting physical and sexual needs, tending plants and gardens and pets, creating clean and neat and safe space, engendering rootedness or sense of place, and mediating interpersonal conflicts and enabling reconciliation—activities all traditionally associated with woman's sphere—these essential and humanizing activities have been undervalued by our Western heteropatriarchy that insists that activities engaged outside the home are more important, more valuable. Plant insists that we need instead to revalue these humane and nurturing activities as we also move away from power hierarchies of domination, exploitation, and exclusion in our larger lives and toward a "decentralization of power" instead, which means

> *moving further and further toward self-governing forms of social organization. The further we move in this direction, the closer we get to what has traditionally been thought of as "woman's sphere"—that is, home and its close surroundings. . . . [Home] is the place where we can learn the values of caring for and nurturing each other and our environments and of paying attention to immediate human needs and feelings.* [8]

More recently, Anne Primavesi has also argued that one's home is a valuable starting place for developing one's ecological and liberational awareness and that one's own ecosystem—spouse, home, yard and garden, pets, neighborhood or section of city, town, or country—is *the* most logical context for interconnecting and theologizing about these issues, [9] as she later elaborates:

> *Rather than. . . reducing work to the pursuit of money and status [a "patriarchal error"], ecofeminists choose to value their interaction with nature. . . because of its importance as a personal relational [subjective] rather than a technical [objective]. . . interconnection with the world. They connect our primary relationship, our home system, with those surrounding us and employing us. They connect these again with the rest of creation.* [10]

As a theologian she goes on to insist that the patriarchal "habit of not situating our relationship to God within the context in which we live must be resisted as unecological. . . [as] damaging to our-selves and the world." [11] In other words, our home is the vital con-text from which springs both our liberational theology and our ecology. As I have already implied, liberation theology and ecology go hand in hand. Julia Scofield Russell extends the metaphorical power of the home to include our daily lives, as these emerge from and return to our home ecosystems, when she acknowledges that "healing the planet begins with us, in our daily lives."[12] In other words,

> *When we consume goods and services without regard for their environmental and social costs, we are supporting technologies and policies that are laying waste to our world. If we resort, or accede, to domination and exploitation in our personal and business lives, we are practicing modes of behavior that are bringing us to the brink of disaster on an international scale.*[13]

How we construct our home ecosystems and how we move out from there in our behavioral relationship to the earth—the biosphere—have global implications. Our individual decisions and actions have a global significance. We cannot wait on larger social or cultural movements to reach fruition before we individually begin to act, whether in liberationally or ecologically sound ways. And revaluing our homes as our sense of place, our nexus or web of life and living relationships, is a vital means for beginning the twofold process of increasing our own awareness and changing our own behavior. Certain seemingly mundane home activities, for example, began my own investment in ecotheology. As my spouse and I began seriously reading the various magazines to which we had subscribed, initially motivated by a rather nebulous and generalized ecological concern, and as we viewed more and more related programs on public television, we began to become increasingly aware and subsequently incensed by the dimensions of the ecological crises facing our earth.[14] How we read and how we watch television changed, as did how we act and how we reflect upon these issues. Over a short period of time, the home-based activities of reading magazines and watching television took on more significant valuational implications for our lives. From the context of our home, we began to reconstruct our ecological behavior and, in that process—from our home as context—we began to see the reflective underpinnings for our own transformed actions. Home thus became the location for further developing a gay liberation *and* an ecologically sensitive theological voice in my own life and work.

FINDING OUR VOICES, ASSERTING OUR AUTHORITY

Just as we cannot wait for the ecology and conservation movements to achieve full political accreditation and power before we begin to act and to advocate in ecologically sound ways—the ecological crises are already too dire—so neither can we wait for institutions to sanction our efforts to theologize in ecologically and liberationally sound ways; their inherent heteropatriarchalism will forever thwart us if we apologetically choose that route. We must instead find our own voice and assert our *assumed* authority to speak to these issues, unabashedly and unapologetically.[15] Ultimately, neither gay men and lesbians, nor women, nor people of color, nor Native Americans, nor any other oppressed people can afford to wait for a white heteromale conferral of authority to speak—neither in politics, nor in theology, nor in ecology. The earth, our home in the broader sense, cannot afford to wait for the status quo's championing. We must assume and assert our own a priori prophetic authoritativeness to "speak from God's point of view."[16] Our authority to speak is borne out of our experience of oppression. Our exclusion as gay men and lesbians in a heteropatriarchal and homophobic ethos in fact stands in judgment of both canon and tradition and explodes their boundaried exclusivity. Moreover, the solidarity of oppression means that as we assert and create our own liberation from exclusion and objectification (our disvaluation as merely sexual, and hence subhuman, beings), so also are we obliged to seek the liberation of other persons, and of the very earth itself, from objectification, devaluation and disvaluation, and exploitation. Our having been consigned by heteropatriarchy to the merely sexual realm of nonhuman or subhuman nature means we share with nature both the urge for liberation from such oppressive categorization and the demand for *re*valuation and justice as right-relation. Consequently, gay ecotheology, as activities, actions, or praxis, cannot depend on divine revelation or any other external, hierarchical "authority." Our praxis must be informed by our experience and our awareness of present conditions and their future implications in relation to all that is and by virtue of the intrinsic value of all that is—not just human beings.

Theologically this means, among other things, that if one is *not* tied a priori to a Christian framework—or is at least willing to call that very framework itself into question—then one's capacity to develop an ecotheological vision is freer and more fluid, better able to range over the entire, two-pronged Judeo-Christian tradition, and over other religious traditions such as those of native America as well. Presuming the rightness or putative superiority of the Christian framework, for example, always risks having that presupposition become a hierarchical, exclusionary value norm. After all, unfortunately, and despite certain prophetic voices to the contrary, mainstream Christianity has most frequently been a religion of the power-holding status quo (i.e., its white, heteromale representatives), including industrialization (and its imperialistic exploitation of peoples and nature) and the objectification of scientific endeavor (and its devaluation of matter and, thence, nature). Any inherent prophetic tension with the status quo in our Western religious tradition has largely been that of disempowered minority voices having little efficacy against the stronger patriarchal ways of thinking and doing. Consequently, we have to learn to read *through* the Christianity of our Christian sources to glean what they have to say that is valuable in unexclusive and liberational ways. Similarly, if Christianity has hopelessly literalized its own metaphors, then we would do well to avoid those now flattened metaphors and generate new metaphors and images instead, because most people cannot reinvigorate the traditional metaphors without falling into the entropic trap of their now centuries-old literalizations.

Our assumption of liberational authority and our willingness to stand outside specifically Christian loyalties enables gay liberation theology and gay ecotheology to bring a fresh critical perspective to even the wisest of extant sources for our reflection. Virtually all ecofeminist writers, for example, unwittingly function under a heterosexist assumption; their feminist analysis is often restricted to man-woman domination and their examination of Genesis assumes that heterosexuality is somehow normative. For others, the Christian preference threatens to create a hierarchy of values that undoes their feminist leveling of such hierarchies. To assume as Anne Primavesi does, for example, that there is a "Christian spirit at the root of the world tree" and to assert that Christianity's primacy can enable us to live ecologically[17] belies a hierarchical value priority that risks placing Christianity over and above other religious perspectives that may be equally or better able to inform an ecological perspective. She must walk a fine line between offering a prophetic corrective word *to* Christianity and speaking *from* Christianity to advocate a Christian paradigm as our best ecological alternative.

Not dissimilarly, James Nash altogether ignores the feminist injunction against hierarchies and tries to do too many contradictory things at once. He tries to work out a theological basis for ecology while insisting upon a hierarchical valuation, again based on an assumed Christian superiority, that arrogantly maintains that, because humans experience and create values, humans are more important than nonhuman nature. His own value hierarchy is of the same utilitarian and anthropocentric sort that inevitably leads to abuses, as a sampling of his statements will illustrate: "Biotic egalitarianism strikes me as a moral absurdity"; the value of other creatures "is not equal to that of humans"; the demand of ecological responsibility is "less rigorous" than the demand of human social justice; ecojustice should not imply equality or deny human primacy; "when conflicts [over environmental rights] occur, and they inevitably do, nonhuman organisms are likely to be the losers —unless there is some reason to respect their existence beyond their instrumental values to humankind."[18] And yet, despite Primavesi's Christian heterosexism and Nash's far worse arrogant anthropocentrism, these writers as well as others offer both analyses and solutions that may prove useful *when first tested against* our own newly asserted authoritative voice on these issues.

ARTICULATING A GAY ECOTHEOLOGICAL PARADIGM

The critical stance already assumed suggests that gay and lesbian experience and theology can contribute something unique to ecological reflection and analysis. Once again our experience of oppression and exclusion, coupled with the silence of even our best sources, constitutes the fundamental rationale for our seizure of the authority to speak, to articulate a gay ecotheological paradigm by which to examine all our sources. While we would not expect the so-called deep ecologists and other heteromale writers, who do not take gender analyses into account anyway, to include our particular perspective, it is surprising that the vast majority of ecofeminist writers do not include gay/lesbian oppression as part of their analysis of human and ecological oppression and exploitation. Even when women, African Americans, Native Americans, and third-world peoples and their environments are acknowledged and examined, gay men and lesbians are consistently absent and invisible.

With great irony we realize that the process of legally and democratically extending rights—first to African Americans, then to women, and to some as yet all-too-limited extent to endangered species and the environment[19]—is nothing but a so-called liberal progression that has conveniently passed over certain groups—most Native Americans, the poor and the homeless, and gay men and lesbians—that are deemed invisible at best and aesthetically or morally undesirable at worst and that therefore remain disenfranchised. These groups of people and all too much of the biosphere as well are, if not invisible even in liberal analyses, treated as devalued, disvalued, and disposable. Disvaluation and disposability not only affect our gay and lesbian lives through antigay/lesbian violence and AIDS apathy but also continue to shape environmental attitudes as well. As a result, our voices must continue to be raised against heteropatriarchy. We must speak against any cultural narrow-mindedness that sanctions antigay/lesbian violence, that sanctions apathetic and even judgmentally punitive attitudes toward

AIDS among gay men, IV-drug users, the poor, and third-world peoples of color, and that also sanctions the exploitation and disposability of the earth.

Primavesi has noted that "by becoming aware of patterns of domination [and exploitation] in our own lives, we learn to connect these patterns with the domination of nonhuman nature."[20] Indeed we do, for we are reminded that the heteropatriarchal dualisms that link nature, women, and sexuality extend to gay and lesbian people who are also viewed as primarily and excessively sexual and unspiritual. We, too, are subject to heteropatriarchy's devaluing and disvaluing reductionism. In fact, our experience of total disvaluation as value*less* (and/or even as "bad") and of violence against us as gay men and lesbians enables us also to see the extent to which heteropatriarchy also disvalues nature and acts violently upon both the human and nonhuman environment. One historical example and one culturally stereotypical example will suffice to illustrate these interconnections.

Ecofeminist historian Carolyn Merchant has argued that the social changes of the early industrial revolution and the shift in worldview from benevolent organicism to impersonal and alienating mechanism made femininely associated nature alien. Real women became the scapegoats, as witches, for the perceived disorder.[21] Today's social upheaval, brought on by the head-on collision of sexual and gender liberation during the 1960s and 1970s with the harsh reality of AIDS in the 1980s and into the 1990s, all occurring at the end of a millennium, has made gay men and lesbians, and other perceived risk groups, into scapegoats. The sixteenth-century fear that "if order were taken away, chaos would reign"[22] today motivates an antigay/lesbian violence that parallels the witch hunts of the earlier period. The focus on sexual lust and passion that condemned the perceived unbridled sexuality of witches and heretics is now turned upon gay people. Just as the witch trials were a symptom of turmoil and social resistance to change,[23] so is today's treatment of gay men, lesbians, and people with AIDS (PWAs).

Witches were believed vulnerable to Satan and capable of passing the demonic to their sexual partners; gay men and lesbians in the military today, for example, are believed vulnerable to the enemy and liable to pass on vital secret information; gay men are believed vulnerable to uncontrollable sexual behavior and somehow held responsible for passing the HIV virus to putatively "innocent" nongay victims. The sixteenth-century witch-trial mentality finds a parallel in our society's AIDS-as-punishment mentality. Finally, Merchant also notes that "not only were the majority of accused persons women [83%], the victims were primarily people in the lowest social orders,"[24] just as the perceived "guilty" among PWAs are gay men, IV-drug users, and African Americans, and third-world peoples whom heteropatriarchy also still views as excessively sexual and somehow less than human, i.e., white heteromale humanity.

Apart from this strict historical analysis, part of the "homosexual threat" to Western heteropatriarchal society is the perception or stereotype that gay men and lesbians opt out of the whole patriarchal system of male control over female reproduction, which Primavesi and other ecofeminists have analyzed.[25] Gay people demonstrate that relationships need not be about the business of controlling procreation or even about the business of procreation at all. Gay and lesbian sexuality, relationships, and where freely chosen, even procreation are not about dominating and controlling (re)production. Although some gay men may do so, they do not need to exploit women and therefore should champion women, all oppressed persons, and the earth. Gay men should eschew all exploitation—of other gay men, sexually or otherwise, and of the earth or nature—and should make sure that we do not play into the stereotype of gay male "expendable income" and its consequent consumerism. This movement from human relational liberation to ecological responsibility is reiterated in the words of Michael Zimmerman:

> From the ecofeminist perspective it makes no sense to speak of caring for nonhuman beings apart from our capacity to care for each other.

The moral context in which we can become concerned about non-human beings is made possible by particular human beings with needs and the capacities to take care of those needs. [26]

In other words, our urge for justice as right-relation for our spouses and friends logically broadens to a concern for right-relation for all people (social justice) and for all the earth (ecojustice). Based upon this understanding, a gay ecotheological paradigm can join as another dimension to the liberational forces already arrayed against those ways of thinking and acting that imperil not only human lives but the whole biosphere as well.

In fact, we may wish to construct our gay liberation ecotheological analysis in contradistinction to that of (hetero)male "deep ecology," and as a further extension of ecofeminism, which has so often remained heterosexist and blind to gay/lesbian oppression. According to deep ecology, an *anthropo*centric worldview of human self-centeredness has led to environmental problems; in contrast, according to ecofeminism, an *andro*centric worldview of masculine privilege and social structures has devalued and exploited both women and nature. [27] Gay ecotheology will insist that both these views are incomplete; the predominantly Western, white, hetero-masculinist worldview is the problem. Not only are women, nature, and sexuality *de*valued, but heteropatriarchy's hierarchy of values and categories *dis*values diversity; reductionism exploits and destroys anyone and anything designated as "other." While eco-feminist analysis involves a "consistent recognition of the limits of hierarchical patterns of thought, of the way in which our culture has been and still is dominated by the questions posed and answers given by a male 'scientific' consciousness," [28] gay ecotheology wants to turn such putative heteromale objectivity inside out and to testify from our experience of oppression (our subjectivity), thus moving beyond the ecofeminist analysis of sexism to an analysis of *hetero*sexism. In other words, what we see is not just a *de*valuing, or *lowering*, of value, which leads to domination and exploitation, but a *dis*valuing, which *strips away* all value and which thereby leads to exclusion, to being disposable, to being acceptable for extinction.

One concrete ecological example can further clarify this distinction: not only has our society and its governmental representatives *de*valued the old-growth forests of the Pacific Northwest, *lowering* their value from something intrinsically valuable in their own right to something valuable only as a natural resource to be exploited for financial gain, but it has also *dis*valued the spotted owl whose habitat these forests provide, assigning it *no* utilitarian value and thereby deeming it expendable. A mindset that understands value only in terms of dollar signs readily accepts the exploitation of the forests for short-term gain as well as the virtual extinction of one species of owl, an extinction that would further weaken an already *dis*valued diversity of life.

This, then, becomes the basis for the uniqueness of our gay voice, another difference, not in opposition to, but a collaborative and creative extension of, feminist analysis. Gay liberation theology has elsewhere noted that while feminist theology adequately deals with issues of human evil and responsibility for oppression, in view of AIDS, gay theology must also wrestle with natural evil and theodicy and thereby synthesize a theology that addresses both human evil (homophobia) and natural evil (AIDS).[29] Likewise, in the ecological arena, gay ecotheology must move beyond the issues of domination and exploitation to those of disvaluation, exclusion, and expendability in order to synthesize a theology that radically celebrates diversity and the intrinsic value of all that is, whether the human, the biospheric, or the geospheric. Ecofeminism has articulately addressed the patriarchal hierarchy of value that *de*values (lowers value) in order to dominate, use, and exploit. Gender roles and sexist exploitation are paradigmatic illustrations. Gay ecotheology must extend this to address the *hetero*patriarchal hierarchy of value that *dis*values (strips of all value) in order to get rid of, to use up, to dispose of as having no further use or no use whatsoever. Exclusion, expendability, and the denial of the value of diversity are paradigmatically illustrative. While ecofeminists work against the devaluation and domination of self and world as utilitarian objects for a masculine society, gay ecotheology must work against the disvaluation and exclusion of self and world as disposable, worthless commodities in a society that disdains diversity and eliminates as unnecessary that which has no utilitarian value.

As gay men and lesbians look out upon our disposable society of planned obsolescence and throw-things-away consumerism, we cannot help but be aware of the growing trash heap, the overburdened land fills, the industrially polluted waters, and the barges bearing the unwanted refuse of the Emerald City, anchored off Manhattan. For us, disvaluation-exclusion-disposability must factor into ecological analysis in addition to devaluation-exploitation-domination, not only because we see our society virtually willing to throw away our earth, our home, but because we carry within our collective memory an awareness of just how often human beings themselves have been treated as expendable and disposable. Heteropatriarchy has historically treated African Americans, Native Americans, the poor and the homeless, the physically and mentally challenged, and virtually all third-world peoples as either expendable after use (in slavery or minimum-wage slavery) or as totally useless. Heteropatriarchy produced a Hitler who considered the Jews totally worthless (immediately expendable via the gas chambers) and gay men of little more value (expendable via the work camps and medical experiments—more heteromale "science" in action). Heteropatriarchy also produced Columbus, whose dubious quintcentenary we have marked, and the subsequent onslaught of Spanish conquistadors and other Europeans upon the Western hemisphere. *Archaeology* magazine recently described the extent to which the indigenous peoples of the Caribbean were treated as disposable after first contact, used as slaves for gold mines and sugar cane plantations, and decimated by disease and execution. When the native Lucayan and Taino populations were decimated by disease and exhausted by forced labor, they were simply replaced by African slaves. Both native islanders and imported Africans were viewed as having no souls and therefore as easily replaceable, expendable.[30] And now, in the wake of the Persian Gulf crisis, it is quickly becoming common knowledge the extent to which our society and our government disvalue the men and women who have served the government's own militaristic ends. Vietnam era and Persian Gulf veterans are among the homeless whom our culture considers disposable, and whom the Veterans Administration too often turns away when homeless and treats inappropriately when ill.

In the history of the gay and lesbian communities, never has our own expendability been so evident as in the rising incidence of antigay/lesbian violence and particularly in the AIDS health crisis. The same heteropatriarchal value hierarchy that insists that nature is reducible to expendable resources also insists on dichotomizing innocent and not innocent (i.e., expendable) victims of AIDS. A decade plus into the AIDS pandemic, our society treated Earvin "Magic" Johnson as if he were the first person ever to become HIV-positive, although portions of our society were quick to dismiss him, too, as a sexually promiscuous person of color. Our government continues to spend money in the pursuit of testing protocols and vaccines, while our politico-medical system still drags its feet in regard to approving treatment protocols or to finding a cure. Gay men, IV-drug users, people of color, and third-world countries where AIDS rages heterosexually are still devalued and/or disvalued. Our expendability mitigates the urgency of cure or treatment. And yet, while the media touted Magic Johnson, in one six-week period my spouse and I lost a dozen friends and acquaintances to death from AIDS while locally another PWA died in isolation in the county jail because the AIDS-insensitive police mistook his AIDS-related dementia for a reckless or even criminal mental condition. We are being treated as expendable objects to be used or found useless and then discarded. To borrow from a set of cultural stereotypes, heteropatriarchy employs gay men to decorate its homes and offices, to choreograph its musical entertainments, to arrange its disposable flowers, to develop and serve its cuisines, to type and file its reports, and to perform a host of other service tasks, in addition to many unstereotypical jobs, but the moment we become sick with AIDS or even infected with HIV, we thereby become useless to heteropatriarchy and we are assigned a scarlet letter A, the new pink triangle of undesirability and disposability. And our experience of expendability becomes the symbol or paradigmatic metaphor of Western culture's attitudes toward all the earth. Hence, our gay ecotheology must adamantly oppose any disvaluation and exclusion that leads to dispensing with diversity and disposing of life. Neither gay men and lesbians, nor the biosphere, nor the geosphere, nor any of the great diversity that god/ess creates and delights in is expendable. Defending the value of diversity and opposing disvaluation and expendability become the foundation of a gay ecotheology.

Remembering as we must, however, that liberation does not entail championing the oppressed-who-can-do-no-wrong,[31] our critical perspective must also include several caveats. Gay men and lesbians must be held accountable whenever we accede to or cooperate with the forces of oppression, exploitation, and expendability. Our ecotheology will challenge any gay/lesbian assimilation that mitigates our difference, our diversity, and it will also call our own lives, particularly our actions as consumers, into scrutiny. For gay men in particular, our ecotheology will also ask that we examine our socialization as men.[32] If ecofeminists have seen that "men in our society are socialized to perceive their identity in opposition to a devalued, female-imaged world,"[33] then we must look to our own lives to discern how we as gay men have been conditioned to accept exploitation, disvaluation, and expendability—worthlessness —in our lives, even when these cultural values are turned against our lives as gay men or as PWAs. Ideally for us, if the typical Western masculine socialization process works against a compassionate, caring, nurturant empathy for nature (anyone and anything not a white, heterosexual, human male), gay men who escaped that socialization process to whatever degree may be able to demonstrate, for all men, a male-embodied love and care for nature, as well as for holistic sexuality and gender role-free relational styles. Potentially, at least, gay men and lesbians together can become the embodied witnesses for an ecotheology of liberation.

Through these reflections we discover that not only do gay liberation theology and gay ecotheology go hand in hand, but also that our theologizing is a process that transforms our vision. We are able to appreciate the degree to which the Emerald City gave us refuge and the freedom to be ourselves, while also realizing the extent to which our lavender ghettos restricted our vision and our participation in the world. Despite our putative safety in numbers, our confrontation with antigay/lesbian violence and with AIDS—our confrontation with our mortality if you will—has led us ever more defiantly to reclaim the value of our lives in the very face of death. Not only has our experience of oppression enabled us to find our voice and to claim our authority to speak, but that very subjectivity has also empowered us to construct a prophetically critical perspective for examining the larger society, the lenses by which we can discern that in our ecological resources that can further enrich our liberational efforts. As we examine these sources and, in doing so, begin to move beyond our ghettos to (re)confront heteropatriarchal abuses and the theological categories that imperil the environment, we can begin to create a gay ecotheology that discloses that our gay and lesbian existence is not only a mode of being-*in*-the-world but also a way of being-*with*-the-world as copartners in the processes of healing and liberation and thereby in the quest for and realization of justice as right-relation throughout the earth.

Paul Bunyan and Other Gods
of Patriarchal Ecocide

The Forest of Real Life is in a desperate condition now because of too many who think too much and care too little. . . . The one chance we have to avoid certain disaster is . . . to learn to value wisdom and contentment. . . . We can no longer afford to look so desperately hard for something in the wrong way and in the wrong place. If Knowledge and Cleverness are allowed to go on wrecking things, they will before much longer destroy all life on earth as we know it.

—Benjamin Hoff, *The Tao of Pooh*

The Patriarchal Bull in a Fragile World

His heavy boots are redolent of leather, grass, and mud; his jeans are sturdy but worn, drawn snug around his massive thighs and crotch; his flannel shirt is sweet with his own musky scent, its sleeves rolled taut over bulging muscles; his tanned face, too, is strong, his sandy moustache is full and his blue eyes are bright. But this is not merely an image of some super Castro clone to make gay men weak in the knees. No, this is Paul Bunyan, a macho image of Americana—woodsman, lumberman, frontiersman, and hero. And yet he is hardly a heroic image for the rainforests, for stripped, eroded, and flooded lands, or even for our own barren, treeless, and dehumanizing suburbs. Feminists would also note that this man's companion and beast of burden (and, as such, his surrogate patriarchal wife) is female—the blue ox Babe. No matter how handsome

21

he might be, for those of us who cherish the trees and the very earth itself, Paul Bunyan is a destructive image of machismo, a god of ecocide. Earlier in our cultural history, we find another equally disturbing male image, Hades, the god of the underworld who annually required that Persephone abandon the earth and join him in Hades. While the male god was annually responsible for the death of nature, the female goddess, Demeter, annually rescued her daughter and together these women restored life to the biosphere.

All too vividly we see, from Greek mythology to frontier Americana, patriarchal images of the (hetero)masculine destruction of the earth. While the whole host of feminist theologians and that gay liberation theology that stems from feminist paradigms have together provided detailed analyses of heteropatriarchy and its relation to theology and faith,[1] these images of patriarchal destruction in the biosphere remind us that we must revisit those analyses as part of the process of creating an ecologically sound theology. On the extremely crippling impact of patriarchy on our ecological attitudes, for example, Brian Swimme has noted, "The patriarchal mind-set of our culture is very similar to a frontal lobotomy. . . . We have only a sliver of our original minds still operative . . . the sliver chiseled to perfection for controlling, for distancing, for calculating, and for dominating."[2] Consequently, on the therapeutic value of reexamining patriarchy's impact in order to begin ecological healing, Julia Scofield Russell has responded that "we must question the entire civilization that [Western patriarchy] has contrived —all of its values, its goals, its achievements. . . . It is antihuman [and] antilife."[3] The wellspring from whence heteropatriarchy draws such power is its inherent tendency to create hierarchies based on value dualisms—superior/inferior, sacred/profane, spirituality/bodiliness-and-sexuality, mind/nature, men/women, heterosexual/homosexual. Value dualisms and value hierarchies permeate a cultural mindset that devalues and exploits, disvalues and excludes.

Not surprisingly, as Nancy Howell has recently realized, there is no empirical grounding for these oppressive structures. She says, "Ecology demonstrates that there is no natural hierarchy governing [either] human society or nature."[4] Hierarchy is itself a construction, a fabrication; not even the reality of the food chain among plants and animals should imply any *value* hierarchy, nor should degrees of perceived intelligence or presumed sentience. In fact, apart from its values, Howell argues, hierarchy would be a harmless intellectual construct; nothing is "inherently wrong with hierarchy. . . . However, value-hierarchical thinking and value dualisms . . . become problematic when coupled with a logic of domination [that creates] an oppressive conceptual framework which justifies and maintains relations of subordination and domination."[5] In other words, hierarchy fails as a fabrication for constructing reality and instead becomes oppressive because of its implicit value—domination. Most unfortunately for all the oppressed, both human and nonhuman, our oppressive heteropatriarchal worldview "no longer recognizes that hierarchy is an ideology [a subjective mental fabrication] and confuses hierarchy with objective reality"; moreover, for a cultural mindset that has so confused ideology with reality, "antihierarchicalism is unimaginable. . . . The planet will probably succumb to our lack of imagination."[6]

The foremost dilemma springing from this failure of imagination, especially in light of our culture's hierarchical dualisms, is the problem of the "other," essentially anyone or anything not identified as a white heterosexual male. Heteropatriarchal consciousness has in fact historically and consistently "denigrated and manipulated everything defined as 'other' whether nature, women, or third world cultures,"[7]—or gay men and lesbians. Ecofeminism has been especially aware of the sexism or misogyny that this alienating category of otherness causes, both for women and, ultimately, for nature as well:

> *Latent misogyny functions. . . [to] create a society in which men keep women mentally and emotionally at arm's length. Women can be exalted as wife, virgin, mother, or deprecated and abused as temptress*

and whore. . . . She is not encountered as a contributing equal to men. . . .

Ecofeminism makes connections between such fragmentation [alienation] of male and female sensibility within human relationships and within attitudes to nature. . . . It connects patterns of male domination of women with those in which science and technology are bound to a conception of absolute mastery over nature.

Ecofeminism stresses the connection between women and nature on the grounds that nature . . . has also been made "other."[8]

As the *dominated* "other," ecofeminists are now reclaiming and re-directing their traditional identification with nature, heretofore construed by patriarchy as a rationale for oppression and exploitation, in fresh and liberating ways. In much the same fashion, as the *excluded* "other," gay men and lesbians have reclaimed the pink triangle and other symbols that affirm our differences, heretofore construed by heteropatriarchy as a rationale for our oppression and expendability, in fresh and liberating ways. Both women and gay people thus affirm diversity, as represented by our difference from the heteropatriarchal norm of procreative, controlled, and dominated sexuality.

As is already evident, the category of otherness inevitably leads to devaluation and disvaluation, to exploitation and exclusion from value (expendability), and to a disdain for diversity, whether among people or within nature. As Primavesi has complained, "The supremacy of images and attitudes of control function . . . as cultural sanctions for the devaluation of nature."[9] And, tragically, when people and nature are devalued, so is diversity, as she subsequently elaborates:

[The] hierarchical imposition of norms embodies a refusal to consider the diversity of creation as a source of joy to [god/ess] and enrichment for the whole systemic creature earth. It presents it instead as a threat. . . . [In contrast,] an ecological system . . . recognize[s] that the greater the diversity of a community, the greater is its resilience and adaptability, and that its survival depends on a balance of diversities, not their elimination.[10]

Heteropatriarchal thinking and valuing constitute a ghettoized mentality whose narrow vision cannot appreciate the richness of various species as intrinsically valuable for their own sake, nor can it appreciate the richness of a diversity of human beings and the kaleidoscope of belief systems, colors, genders, and sexualities. Because the multifaceted quality of life only threatens heteropatriarchy, our culture responds with images and attitudes of putative supremacy, control, and dominion-over. Ynestra King articulately summarizes this destructive mindset when she notes that "a rationalized worldview . . . asserts that human science and technology are inherently progressive, . . . systematically denigrates ancestral cultures [and thereby their wisdom], and . . . asserts that human beings are entitled to dominion over nonhuman nature."[11]

Ultimately, the combined concepts of otherness and dominion-over function to objectify the dominated "other" as a merely utilitarian resource, whether human or nonhuman. "There is no respect for the 'other' in patriarchal society," writes Judith Plant. "The other, the object of patriarchal rationality, is considered only insofar as it can benefit the subject."[12] What emerges, then, in the heteropatriarchal mindset is a "utilitarian attitude," an assumption that "all objects external to human beings . . . are 'passive,' 'inert,' 'inanimate,' that is, that they have neither consciousness, value, nor purpose in themselves. They are there solely . . . to be used for our benefit and 'managed by us,' "[13] and, as we have begun to realize from our gay ecotheological point of view, ultimately also thrown away by us. Cross utilitarianism uses natural resources and human beings themselves as if they are endlessly replaceable and utterly expendable. Trees become paper which becomes trash. When the Spanish decimated the natives of the Caribbean islands, they replaced them with African slaves. When gay men in service occupations become HIV-positive or too sick with AIDS to work, they are replaced and sent away to die—expendable!

And, of course, use breeds abuse; utilitarianism leads to consumerism, which in turn demands more and more and more, myopically blind to the reality that ours is a finite earth—its resources are not limitless. Now, just as AIDS forces a heteropatriarchal culture, which mistakenly acts as if the "right people" are immortal, to face its mortality, so must ecofeminism, gay ecotheology, and other ecological voices compel this same myopic mindset to realize the finitude of the earth. The fruits of utilitarianism are overextension and an ecosphere bled dry, gasping for life. As James Nash has noted, "The ecological crisis is a result of imperialistic overextension—abusing what is divinely intended for [necessary subsistence], subduing far beyond the point of necessity, imaging despotism rather than [responsibility], and failing to nurture benevolently and justly nature's potential hospitality."[14]

The developing Western mindset has completely objectified the whole realm of nature and far too many peoples as well. We have no "thou" relationships with nature, with diverse peoples, or with diverse cultures and belief systems. The progression from otherness to domination, overextension, and expendability has led to alienation, and that growing sense of alienation causes us to wonder about the value of our own lives. Despite the protestations from Christians that they love the sinner and only hate the sin, religiously fed homophobia and AIDS-phobia have certainly compelled lesbians, gay men, and all persons living with HIV and AIDS to question the value of their lives. That we adamantly do value and celebrate our lives, even in the face of death, lies at the heart of gay liberation theology.[15] Just as alienation mitigates any good will offered gay people by institutional religion, so alienation also mitigates our protestations of care for the earth. We claim to love the earth, but we have allowed ourselves no "thou" relationship with nature, and our exploitation of the earth has left us preciously little to love.

In mid-nineteenth-century America the single individual who was most clearly aware of this already growing sense of alienation from nature was Henry David Thoreau. On our protestations of love for nature, for example, he quipped, "There is plenty of genial love of nature, but not so much of nature herself."[16] He saw through our pretense of love for nature, with humor laced with justifiable contempt: "While almost all [people] feel an attraction drawing them to society, few are attracted strongly to nature. In their reaction to nature [people] appear to me for the most part, notwithstanding their arts, lower than the animals. It is not often a beautiful relation."[17] In a period just before our nation was ravaged by a civil war that plundered a great deal of nature itself and extorted vast amounts of resources, both human and nonhuman, Thoreau was particularly aware of the alienation from nature that urbanization was already nurturing. He bemoaned, "Here is this vast, savage, howling mother of ours, nature, lying all around, with such beauty, and such affection for her children... and yet we are so early weaned from her breast to society, to that culture which is exclusively an [human] interaction."[18] Perhaps most of all, Thoreau realized that even then, prior to 1860, the progression of Western culture was already working to turn the whole earth into a ghetto, a wasteland: "Nowadays almost all... improvements, so called, as the building of houses, and the cutting down of the forest and of all large trees, simply deform the landscape, and make it more and more tame and cheap."[19] Implicit in Thoreau, and throughout our other sources as well, is the realization that, between Hades and Paul Bunyan, patriarchy has deepened its stranglehold on the earth. Moreover, two great movements—first Christianity and later the transformation from an organic to a mechanistic view of nature—have joined the ecocidal force of patriarchy to help devastate the earth. Both of these villainous compatriots merit more detailed examination.

THE CHRISTIANIZATION OF THE WEST

Historically, the synthesis of Judaism and Christianity, as a two-pronged and evolving tradition, with the dualisms and value hierarchies of Hellenistic philosophy produced what we have come to recognize as the patriarchal mentality of (hetero)male supremacy.

The offspring of the peculiar marriage of imperialistic Christianity with the ideas of Plato and Aristotle is a mindset that clearly devalues and dominates the biosphere in order to exploit its material "resources" while ultimately disvaluing the material world as a whole in order to achieve spiritual transcendence.[20] As a result, traditions outside Christianity cannot help but perceive so-called traditional Christian values as ecologically destructive ones that have made little positive contribution to our current ecological dilemma.[21] Even an ardent defender of Christianity such as James Nash must finally admit that "Christianity has done too little to discourage and too much to encourage . . . exploitation."[22]

Christianity's destructive force has in fact most often been directed at those other traditions and peoples who have all too clearly witnessed Christianity's ecological and human recklessness. Early Euro-Americans, for example, were incapable of perceiving the spiritual qualities of indigenous Americans and their holistic, interdependent "mysticism of the land" and, as Thomas Berry has noted, "the attack on these qualities by Christians constitutes one of the most barbaric moments in Christian history. This barbarism turned upon the tribal peoples was [subsequently] loosed also upon the American earth with a destructive impact."[23] Unfortunately, this Christian commitment to the despiritualization (or secularization) of nature and indigenous peoples cannot be safely assigned to the historical past alone; Christianity's exploitative, secularizing force continues unabated today: "The greed that motivated the displacement of all indigenous peoples from their lands of spiritual rootedness is the same greed that threatens the destruction of the earth and the continued oppression of so many peoples."[24]

The most articulate voice on these issues in more recent literature is that of Anne Primavesi, who is able to speak as an ecofeminist Christian from within the very tradition that she also prophetically addresses. As a feminist she recognizes that the "god of Christianity . . . appears to be perpetually on the side of the dominant male" and that, as such, "ecclesiastical colonizers" treated indigenous peoples scandalously "on the grounds that they were less than human, or 'soulless.'" [25] Traditional Christianity has consistently honored only one category of persons, the redeemed or the potentially redeemable. It has treated other people and the material world altogether as beyond redemption and, therefore, as having little if any value. Christianity's value hierarchy and otherworldly dualism have perpetuated the oppression and exploitation of all things and beings not included among the select saved. This emphasis on saved human souls opposes diversity—whether of thought, sexuality, or life forms—and values the biosphere only as a means to an end—human spiritual survival into a new and putatively better world. As Primavesi says, "The notion of Christian separateness from the world surfaces as the source of its ecological apartheid," whereas feminism insists instead that "the earth is to be valued for its own sake." [26]

The result of Christianity's false dichotomy of god versus world is that the world has been devalued as not worth knowing. As Nancy Howell noted earlier, mistaking ideology for reality means, in Primavesi's words, that "Christians take the supposedly divine hierarchical structuring of cosmic reality as justification for unecological attitudes to nature," from which "it seemingly follows that God has nothing to do with dirt, sex, natural functions, or anything which connects us to the animal world or the earth"; moreover, for Christians the natural world remains only "a vast and infinitely resilient reservoir" of material resources at the bottom of patriarchy's hierarchy of values, resources that have "no intrinsic worth, only instrumental value." [27] Christianity's hierarchical values and inherent utilitarianism also led to a concept of divine power that was and is "linked to the image of government through force. Relationship to divinity became defined in terms of the dynamics of hierarchical relationships of [imperialistic] power"; in other words, Christianity's urge toward domination and control became manifest as "power-over." [28] Christian power-over has been used historically against women (as witches), against indigenous peoples everywhere (as heathens), and against gay men and lesbians (as sexual heretics); it has been employed to exploit nature and human beings, disposing of both whenever they fail to submit to domination or whenever they no longer hold utilitarian value.

As damning as this picture is, however, attacking Christianity as the solitary patriarchal villain of ecocide is simplistic. Because simplistic analyses usually produce simplistic solutions doomed to failure, we must concede to James Nash that the complaint against Christianity is to some extent "an overgeneralization. It tends to reduce the explanation of the complex ecological crisis to a single cause [and] to exaggerate the authority of Christianity in cultures."[29] He later adds that "ecological crises are not peculiar to Christian. . . cultures. Non-Christian cultures have also caused severe or irreplaceable harm to their ecosystems"; "the near universality of ecological problems suggests that the roots of the crisis are not in theological affirmations. . . but rather in human character."[30] As one example, and contrary to our preferred idealization of "indigenous peoples," Nash argues that, while small indigenous communities may appear to live in equilibrium with their environments, if they grow in numbers and develop technical skills, they too are likely to pursue avenues that lead to ecological problems.[31]

Clearly, any hierarchical religion, belief system, or mindset—whether theocentric or anthropocentric—will devalue and ultimately exploit the material world, but Nash is correct in his observation that some indigenous peoples have used up their immediate environments and moved on to exploit new ones. In recently describing continental native North America before first contact with Europeans, for example, *Smithsonian* magazine contends that local agricultural and/or hunting practices frequently exhausted soils and herds to such an extent that groups of people were forced to abandon their native portions of the earth as an expendable and replaceable commodity.[32] Similarly, Charles Hudson has described the "paleo-Indian population" as a population front that swept across and saturated North America during a five- to eight-hundred-year period, using plant and animal resources with deleterious effects: the mammoth, horse, and camel had become extinct in North America by 9,000 to 8,000 B.C.E.[33] He also notes that,

> contrary to popular opinion, many parts of the Southeast were not virgin forest when Europeans first arrived. The Indians actually modified the forest cover far out of proportion to their number. They repeatedly burned off large portions of the forest to create grazing lands, artificially stimulating the number of deer.[34]

Elsewhere outside Christianity, the recent Persian Gulf crisis further demonstrated the extent to which patriarchal mindsets other than Christianity also wreak havoc on the earth. With seeming impunity, Sadaam Hussein engaged in environmental terrorism as his minions released oil into the gulf, oil that permeated the coastline, not only killing life within the water and along the shore but also torturously killing the various waterfowl that became trapped in the ooze as they searched for food. Furthermore, his soldiers also burned Kuwaiti oil into the atmosphere and used the animals in the Kuwait City zoo for target practice. In the history of the earth, no other single patriarch has ever been responsible for such unmitigated environmental destruction.[35]

Apparently, just as Christianity cannot naively and dualistically be cast in the role of solitary patriarchal villain opposite totally innocent indigenous peoples or other non-Christians, so neither can capitalism be simplistically cast villainously opposite certain alternatives. As we have increasingly come to appreciate the extent of the ecological and economic devastation rampant throughout what were until recently communist Eastern European countries, we must also realize in a qualified sense that Nash is right when he says, "Capitalism is not in itself the cause of the ecological crisis. . . . Every economic system must be restrained, as contemporary forms of ecologically debilitating socialism well illustrate."[36] In short, Christianity alone is not solely to blame; Christianity is one primary villainous force or demon among others. The deeper reverberations of heteropatriarchy and its hierarchical value dualisms include more problematic forces than Christianity alone, although we should never lose sight of the fact that these forces have consistently gone hand in hand with the spread of Christian imperialism, society, and culture:

> The major factors in the emergence of anti-ecological attitudes and actions [also include] population pressures, the development of expansionist capitalism in the forms of commercialism and industrialism. . . , the triumph of Cartesian mechanism in science [objectification]. . . , and the triumph of Francis Bacon's notions of dominion as mastery over nature. [37]

THE GOD OF THE MACHINE

At one level, our heteropatriarchal heritage is clearly that of the western European Christian exploitation of everybody and everything, especially as this heritage has come to fruition in the Americas. The white, heterosexual, Christian, Euro-American male towers paradigmatically over all things and peoples designated as "other." And yet, it is not just his Christianity that is ecologically dangerous. The heteropatriarchal category of otherness is epitomized in the god of the machine, in an alienated mechanistic worldview that objectifies everything. And, as Charlene Spretnak has reminded us, the roots of this mechanism predate even the Christianity that has so readily become its more than willing compatriot:

> Deep ecologists write that our estrangement from nature began with classic Greek humanism and the rise of Judaeo-Christian culture. But ecofeminists say, actually, it began around 4500 [B.C.E.] with the Indo-European invasions of nomadic tribes from the Eurasian steppes, who replaced the nature-based and female-honoring religion of the goddess. . . with their thunderbolt god, removing that which is held sacred and revered from the life processes of the earth to the distant realm of an omnipotent male sky-god. [Earlier than Judeo-Christianity or the scientific revolution, then] one finds the earliest sources of desacralized nature [and] the foundation of a mechanized worldview. [38]

The slow progression of heteropatriarchy toward objectification and mechanization, born this long ago and later wedded to the imperialistic power-over of Christianity, came to a boiling point six millennia later and shook the very foundations of Western culture between 1500 and 1700 C.E. More than a decade since it was first published, Carolyn Merchant's *The Death of Nature* remains the classic, authoritative study of this period of turmoil.[39]

Merchant reminds us, first of all, that technological advances themselves began before any changes in imagery or cultural metaphors occurred that later so strongly reinforced objectification. Over an extended period of time, nascent developing imagery superseded the old imagery and then became the cultural and intellectual sanctions for further "progress" and exploitation. Losing the old images meant also losing important restraints upon the exploitation and abuse of the earth. Says Merchant, "Whereas the nurturing earth image can be viewed as a cultural constraint restricting the types of socially and morally sanctioned human activities allowable with respect to the earth, the new imagery of mastery and domination functioned as cultural sanctions for the denudation of nature"; moreover, while the "pervasive animism of nature [had] created a relationship of immediacy with the human being [before 1500 C.E. that] could effectively function as a restraining ethic," now, as people saw nature being increasingly manipulated by mining, deforestation, and other technologies, their appreciation of the organic integrity of the world was undermined.[40] Although the organic cultural metaphor had been "sufficiently integrative" to account for modest commercial and technological advances for centuries, the rapid acceleration of technological change and its subsequent social change during the period 1500 to 1700 C.E. undermined the viability of that worldview. Organic values no longer fit the mechanization of experience and, as a result, the organic conceptual framework began to deteriorate. As people increasingly experienced the earth and nature (and women) as passive and manipulable, nature (and women) became ripe for exploitation.[41]

While Merchant argues that we "need to develop technologies

that harmonize with natural cycles rather than exploit resources," she also recognizes how fundamentally exploitation has historically shaped human behavior; early on, the "transition from peasant control of natural resources for the purpose of subsistence to capitalist control for the purpose of profit" immediately affected the quality of the environment through mining, through the overuse of the forests for industry, and through the urbanization and industrialization of cities.[42] As people increasingly experienced nature as altered and manipulated—as the further development of technological advances, the development of democracy and individual rights to property, and the development of capitalist institutions all became dependent upon exploiting natural resources—people also experienced an alienation from any immediate organic relationship with nature and, progressively, an alienation in their relationships with other people as well. As communal property became the market resources for monetary exchanges, economic and technological changes impacted the environment while urbanization and increased mobility impacted the social structure. The same forces that were acting to shift cultural metaphors and images were also disrupting ecosystems and thereby affecting people to such an extent that the resulting social upheaval would also change history.[43] Summarizes Merchant, "Models of organic society and modes of social organization were likewise being undermined and transformed."[44]

As mechanism progressively sanctioned the manipulation and exploitation of nature, the residual influence of organicism could only shape ecological and social ethics that were based on a managerial approach to natural (and human) "resources." This "managerial approach to conservation" was and is purely anthropocentric and utilitarian; no *intrinsic* value is accorded to nonhuman nature while human managers assume divine sanction for their exploitative "stewardship."[45] Although we need a "community-oriented ecocentric alternative to the homocentric ethics of ecosystem management," what has actually happened is that "the mechanical framework . . . of power and control sanctioned the management of both nature and society."[46] In other words, the active images of mechanization and management further exacerbated the sexist and heterosexist aspects of heteropatriarchy. In the context of the multidimensional transition from an organic to a mechanistic worldview, the nurturing good-mother image was displaced by the chaotic devouring-mother image. Manipulative and exploitative control was pitted against the uncontrollable elements and the disorder that nascent science revealed were existing in nature; on the human level, because women and "sexual heretics" such as gay men and lesbians represented embodied chaos to a frightened society in transition, witch hunts resulted.[47]

Today this same undaunted mindset allows women to be harassed in the workplace, abused by their spouses, and virtually raped without consequence by any man, while it also encourages antigay/lesbian violence and victim-blaming directed at all persons with AIDS. Managerial ethics, science, and (hetero)sexism still go hand in hand. Merchant describes this (hetero)sexist "ideology of objectivity" when she says, "The new image of nature as a female to be controlled and dissected through experiment legitimated the exploitation of natural resources"; moreover, the "bold sexual imagery... of the modern experimental method—constraint of nature in the laboratory, dissection by hand and mind, and the penetration of hidden secrets—language still used today in praising a scientist's 'hard facts,' 'penetrating mind,' or the 'thrust of his argument'... [linguistically sanctions and] legitimates the exploitation and 'rape' of nature."[48]

As science and (hetero)sexism emerged as the sanctioned mindset of the god of the machine toward the end of this transitional period, order was reachieved by the mechanistic imagery of objectification, by the "Baconian doctrine of dominion over nature" represented by scientific managerial ethics,[49] and, later, by the hierarchicalism of Darwinian evolutionary theory.[50] Thomas Berry has recently described the latter as giving rise to the every*man* for *him*self attitude that still plagues our society today when he notes, "The natural tensions with the earth were increased by the Darwin-

ian principle of natural selection, indicating that the primary attitude of each individual and each species is for its own survival *at the
expense of others.*"[51] Because nature was now understood as inert,
moved not by internal forces but by external manipulation, the mechanical mindset sanctioned the exploitation of nature and the
control of both nature and society. The self became the rational
master of the passions and of sexuality, now separated from, rather
than harmoniously integrated into, nature.[52] Anyone refusing to be
subject to such self-control, whether women, gay men and lesbians, or indigenous peoples of color, became less than human and
thereby exploitable and expendable. Merchant has articulately
elaborated:

> Order was redefined to mean the predictable behavior of every
> part within a rationally determined system of laws, while power derived
> from. . . intervention in a secularized world. Order and power together
> constituted control. . . over nature, society, and the self.
> . . . The death of the world soul and the removal of nature's
> spirits helped to support increasing environmental destruction by
> removing any scruples that might be associated with the view that
> nature was a living organism.[53]

Overall, while this two-century period saw "the transition from the
organism to the machine as the dominant metaphor binding together the cosmos, society, and the self into a single cultural reality
[or] worldview," wherein the metaphor of mechanism came to entail dominion and mastery over both people and nature, Merchant's work as a whole testifies to our needs both to reappraise an
organic worldview that is resistant to the ever-increasing exploitative mentality and to (re)learn to live "within the cycles of nature, as opposed to the exploitative, linear mentality of forward
progress."[54] And Merchant is not alone in her response to this
history.

Mechanism and objectification, exploitation and control of
the earth, are clearly not our only alternatives. Although human
beings can certainly do more than our share of damage to other

people and the environment, we are not in fact "in control" of nature; most certainly, "the earth does not revolve around humankind."[55] Anne Primavesi offers a similar ecofeminist view:

> The proper [patriarchal] attitude . . . sees all sides of an argument and takes none [so-called "objectivity"]. In contrast, a subjective response to the earth . . . leaves us free to express our hopes and fears in language and actions which are discounted in patriarchy as . . . intuitive, bodily, illogical, emotional, and disordered. . . . It is intended to counteract [divide] beings into things and persons, with things to be used and only persons to be respected.[56]

Riane Eisler writes in the same spirit as Primavesi with a historical perspective broader than, but still much like, Merchant's. Based on the best archaeological data available to date, she has further realized that a dramatic change "occurred in our prehistory from an egalitarian and peaceful way of living to the violent imposition of male dominance"; however, she is quick to add that "the real alternative to patriarchy is not matriarchy, . . . the other side of the dominator coin. The alternative [is] a *partnership* society: a way of organizing human relations in which . . . diversity is *not* equated with inferiority or superiority."[57] Eisler is working toward a new synthesis that moves beyond the dialectic of organicism and mechanism and that, pertinent to the caveat discussed earlier, does not simplistically blame either theology or science alone for our ecological dilemmas:

> The basic issue is not one of technology versus spirituality or nature versus culture. The fundamental issue is how we define [these terms]—which in turn hinges on whether we orient to a dominator or a partnership model of society.
>
> It is not science and technology, but the numbing of our innate human sensibilities that makes it possible for men to dominate, oppress, exploit.[58]

Indeed, Eisler is correct; the empirical demand implicit in environmental destruction and ecological crises, as well as the prophetic urgency of liberation theology—and thereby of our gay ecotheology as well—is to move away from blame toward healing and restorative action or praxis, important concerns that merit detailed explication. In the present context, however, the historical overview provides important perspective. The marriage of convenience of patriarchy and mechanism have affected religious doctrines, even as Christianity has also shaped the determining cultural metaphors of mechanism and dominion-over. The more salient of these doctrines, too, must be examined before our historical overview is complete enough to enable us to move on toward reconstructing a gay ecotheology that most fully heals our theological vision and most adequately facilitates our ecologically sound praxis.

THE INTERPLAY WITH RELIGIOUS DOCTRINES

One of the theological places where we can most clearly see the interplay of Christianity, patriarchy, and mechanism as exploitation is in the Genesis creation stories. Christian interpretations of these narratives and their motifs of dominion (power-over) and stewardship (management) have shaped patriarchal, mechanized exploitation even as the patriarchal and mechanized mentality has read itself back into these scriptures. Because the theological concept of dominion is in fact usually "interpreted and enacted as domination," Paul Santmire has recently suggested that "it may be best to call a moratorium on the use of that conceptuality altogether." He goes on to add that "likewise,... the idea of stewardship... may not be worth the effort... to interpret it 'the right way,' since it is so tainted with the nuances of manipulation and exploitation."[59] More straightforward in her similar appraisal, Martha Ellen Stortz argues that the biblical concept of dominion, as set forth in Genesis, has historically served only to justify "human domination of nature. This scripturally based domination then fed into a mechanistic view of nature and aligned itself all too easily with the scientific and industrial revolutions [resulting in the] outright exploitation of nature and [the] onerous oppression by humans of nature."[60] The very notion of dominion sounds patriarchal and hierarchical, a concept that clearly sets human beings over against nonhuman nature; therefore, the concept of dominion cannot entail cooperative caring among beings of equal value and status. At its best, "dominion has narrow implications," admits James Nash. "It is primarily the protection of the planet and its inhabitants *by* humans *against* human exploitation."[61]

The human egocentrism in the concept of dominion is thus painfully clear, as Charlene Spretnak has bluntly noted: "We are entangled in the hubris of the patriarchal goal of dominating nature."[62] Such anthropocentric entanglement invariably leads to abuse and exploitation: "If nature is interpreted mainly in terms of human being, then the spirit of domination, the rape of nature, cannot easily be kept at bay."[63] Overall, then, the traditional, narrow reading of Genesis inherently places "man above woman and nature and legitimate[s] this supremacy in the name of God. It [also describes sexuality] as essentially . . . domination"; moreover, by this reading, Genesis also describes work as a curse, mandates subduing matter (nonhuman nature), and separates immanence (god/ess' intimate presence within the earth here and now) from transcendence (spirituality and otherworldly hopes).[64]

Because in this scripturally based view people are presumed to have the greatest value apart from the divine, cosmically speaking, and are assumed to be in control, the concept of stewardship is the logical correlate of dominion. Influenced by the mechanistic worldview, "stewardship" becomes synonymous with the egotistical management mentality and with that mentality's inherent speciesism, which *always* favors the human over all else. In fact, "speciesism seems implicit in [all] biblical models of stewardship."[65] Stewardship still presumes a hierarchically paternalistic attitude toward the earth and its nonhuman inhabitants. As an operative value, stewardship may eschew exploitation—only whenever such prudence does not interfere with human needs and wants—but it still places humanity at the top of a value hierarchy with nature below as instrumentally but never intrinsically valuable. Or, as Primavesi has said, "Stewardship conveys . . . the notion of anthropocentric and instrumental management of the biosphere as humanly owned 'property' and 'resources.'" As functionaries of management, therefore, "stewards seek to optimize profits for themselves or their bosses. Healers [in contrast] seek to restore their own integrity as part of, not apart from, the integrity of the land. The model of stewardship is unecological."[66]

As a Christian ecofeminist, Primavesi wants to counter both the anthropocentrism and the androcentrism of the traditional dominion-and-stewardship reading of the Genesis materials. Respectively, she argues both that "ecological humility helps counteract the impulse to elevate the human above all other species" (versus anthropocentrism) and that "maleness needs to be reconnected with being grounded in the natural world" (versus androcentrism).[67] Her feminist concern with maleness ultimately leads her to a liberating reconstruction of the meaning of the Hebrew terminology in the creation stories themselves:

> The term 'adam *tells us that the essence of human life is not its eventual classification into gendered [and hierarchical] categories but rather its organic connection to the earth . . .* 'adamah, *that reddish brown substance that is capable of absorbing water, being cultivated, and supporting life.*[68]

Her overall desire to salvage the Genesis material for the believing Christian leads her to affirm that although "the interpretation of the Genesis texts . . . which prevailed was a male construct bound by and acceptable to . . . a patriarchal culture and specific to a time when male consciousness was taken as the norm," nonetheless, an ecofeminist alternative reading is also possible: "The integral relationship between sustenance, the difficulties of securing it, and human relations," all depicted as interwoven in Genesis, "are the interpretive grid though which, . . . ecology reminds us, this narrative has become relevant today."[69]

James Nash and other ecologists also want to salvage the Genesis materials. Focusing not upon the creation narratives but upon the subsequent flood story, they insist that the covenant with

Noah, or rainbow covenant, portrays the divine as "making an unconditional pledge in perpetuity to all humanity, to all other creatures, and to the earth itself, to preserve *all* species and their environments," but because the "ecological covenant" entailed by the Noahide covenant "assumed responsibilities to future generations of humanity," ecological abuses in the present violate this ongoing covenant.[70] The rainbow covenant was established between the divine and every living thing, including the earth itself as well as human beings. As a result, it actually contravenes anthropocentric hubris. According to Philip Hefner, the rainbow signifies that god/ess will never "permit that covenant to be breached in favor of humans at the expense of the earth," because god/ess is *the* advocate for nonhuman nature; a human spirituality that acknowledges such advocacy would be "a spirituality of human solidarity with nature," a spirituality that reaffirms the fundamental interrelatedness of divine-human-nature rather than sustaining the alienation of divine, human, and nature that invariably leads to exploitation.[71]

Any problems inherent in any of these views may be seen as the result of these writers' presuppositions, their assumption of an imputed authority in the Genesis materials. As we have seen, both gay liberation theology and gay ecotheology reject the need to appeal to any such outside authorities. For example, to read Genesis chapters 1 through 3 as a story of origins with at least two primary motifs—that male dominion, stewardship, or domination of nature is somehow divinely decreed and that "original sin" came into human existence by means of putatively "evil" nature (represented by the serpent and imputed to all women)—is clearly to engage in a (hetero)patriarchal and (hetero)sexist reading-back into a historical text. However, Primavesi's ecofeminist alternative—that in context the story is about the conditions of life at the time, the struggle for basic subsistence, and the paradox of a very difficult existence being given by a presumably loving god—may be wishful thinking that is, at best, also a reading-back into the text and, at worst, still a heterosexist reading.

Even if the archetypal man and woman *are* created equal, the gender roles of procreative necessity are still a very significant part of the human survival message in this text, a dialectic that still pits men and women together in a struggle against nature (as resistant "other") in order to survive. Human domination of nature is still implicit because the bottom line is that humans are the pinnacle of creation and must survive, come what may. Obviously, the Genesis creation narratives do not clearly present an ecological view and, by virtue of their heterosexist assumption, however historically necessary it might be in context, have little if anything to say to gay men and lesbians—except to remind us all of our inherent connection to the earth, to 'adamah. The question remains, do we have to resort to Genesis or to any scripture for a sound ecotheological vision? Our gay ecotheology will affirm that we do not; our experience of oppression and expendability, and of that reflected in our culture's exploitative and disposable attitudes toward the earth, as well as our experience of god/ess' intimate nearness and co-empowerment, are surer groundings for our liberational ecotheology. Given that assertion, the conclusion of the flood narrative does have at least anecdotal value for our gay ecotheology. If gay and lesbian people are truly a "rainbow people," celebrating our own diversity, as signified by our rainbow flag, and celebrating the earth's diversity as well, then our encounter with and appreciation of the rainbow covenant in Genesis 9 again reminds us that we must not seek some otherworldly, ghettoized, "over the rainbow" panacea, but must instead honor the rainbow covenant in solidarity with all other oppressed persons, with god/ess, *and* with the earth, intimately interrelated here and now.

Unfortunately, the fact that such divine immanence has more often been overshadowed by transcendence is the other significant religious confluence of patriarchy, Christianity, and mechanism that we must examine. The dangers that an overemphasis on transcendent spirituality and eschatological otherworldliness pose for human liberation have been articulately discussed by both feminist and gay liberation theologies elsewhere.[72] In the context of ecology, however, we are again reminded of the extent to which transcendent, otherworldly spiritualities devalue and disvalue this life and this material, earthly world. As Catherine Keller has noted, the "drive to transcendent unity" with the divine, outside or beyond this life and this world, is "a profound impetus in all patriarchal spirituality, and it always achieves its end at the expense of nature and multiplicity."[73] Devaluing this earth inevitably leads to the careless disvaluing of the diversity of life on earth by means of exploitation to the point of the extinction of species. Eliminating complexity works toward eliminating any viable future for life on earth—a matter of little concern, unfortunately, for the apocalyptically minded, as Keller also observes: "Apocalypticism portrays the death of everything as the way to the eternal life of the privileged few."[74]

The real danger beneath transcendent, eschatological spirituality becomes frighteningly clear: not only does such spirituality disvalue and disdain the earth, but the linear thinking that informs such spirituality actually looks forward to the total demise of the earth. The danger of patriarchal, linear thinking is that it assumes both a literal beginning ("creation") and a literal ending ("eschaton"). Coupled with a transcendent, otherworldly spirituality, such linear thinking also implies that we can or should work the earth to that end and thereby hasten the arrival of the "next" world. Such otherworldliness not only devalues and disvalues this world but actually sanctions exhausting a clearly expendable earth. In response to such thinking, therefore, Keller has not only acknowledged that "the expectation of an end-time and of an end of time has . . . defined the limits of western patriarchal consciousness" but has also realized that neither "scientific modernity" with its seemingly endless exploitation of "resources" nor religious apocalypticism "reflects the spatiotemporal rhythms of earthly ecology."[75]

Clearly, neither patriarchal religion (Christianity) nor patriarchal mechanism (science) respects the earth to the extent necessitated by current ecological crises. As we might expect, therefore, feminists and ecofeminists have been quick to respond and to extend Keller's insights. Anne Primavesi, for example, challenges any linear thinking that either disvalues this world generally or that does so in anticipation of a messianic redemption of nature coming from outside this life and this world: "Ecology does not consider this world and our lives and relationships in it as of relative value to our continued existence in another world with God. It does not expect direct answers to its problems from God, or . . . divine revelation . . . [or] divine intervention."[76] That the responsibility for redeeming the earth is clearly upon our shoulders in the radical here and now of god/ess' immanent presence with us and not something that we can defer until some transcendent eschaton is consistent with both feminist and gay liberation theology. The demand of radically present praxis challenges linear thinking and revalues the cycles of the earth and of life here and now, as Rosemary Radford Ruether contends when she insists, "One has to disrupt the linear concept of order to create a different kind of order that is truly the way nature 'orders,' that is, balances and harmonizes. . . . Converting our minds to the earth means understanding the more diffuse and relational logic of natural harmony."[77]

Carol Johnston undertakes just such reordering when she reconceptualizes the final depiction of apocalypticism in Scripture, envisioning not a linear endpoint but a present image toward which we might direct our praxis. She argues that the apocalypse as depicted in Revelation chapters 21 to 22 portrays the divine as coming to dwell with people on earth. Rather than forsaking the earth as an expended commodity, her view affirms the earth as *the* locus of intimate and healing divine presence and companionship: "In this vision, it is not earth that will be abandoned, but heaven. . . . This is a metaphorical vision of shalom, imaging a world of restored trust. God, human beings, and earth are reunited and dwell together in peace [with] the flourishing diversity of creation."[78] Whether such hopeful scriptural reconstruction and revisioning can counter popular disposable-style eschatology is, of course, an open question.

Because the patriarchal and linear mentality is not merely a religious matter, transcendence in our culture has not been restricted to traditional eschatological spirituality. The secular and scientific side of the mechanistic confluence has also provided transcendent or escapist possibilities that equally disvalue the earth as an expendable resource. Yaakov Garb, for example, has realized that our fascination with extraterrestrials in science fiction and our space explorations (whose billions of dollars are funded while the earth languishes and people go hungry) are nothing less than "oversized literalization[s] of the masculine transcendent ideal, . . . attempt[s] to achieve a self-hood freed not only from gravity but from all it represents: the pull of the earth, of matter, [of] the body."[79] Just as human beings refuse to confront and accept their limits and their mortality by indulging in eschatological spiritual hopes, so do we also refuse to acknowledge our limits and the earth's limits by implicitly pursuing "goals of radical independence and autonomy from embeddedness in the natural world" through technology (machines) that is increasingly "costly and life-threatening."[80] In transforming the patriarchal god "out there" into a secularized panacea at some distance from our planet, our home, we have perpetuated the notion that the whole earth can be disposed of without harm to the human species, as if we can just go on and plunder and exploit our way infinitely throughout the whole universe with impunity. After all, our own planet is already surrounded by orbiting space trash. Why not the whole cosmos? Garb recognizes that this is accurately the extent to which secularized transcendent escapism can lead when he concludes that from outer space "we see the earth outgrown, transcended, and discarded, a worn and spent relic from humanity's childhood that can be trashed as we move on."[81]

Overall, then, James Nash is correct *up to a point*; our theological deconstruction of ecological crises is far from simple. Neither patriarchy, nor Christianity, nor mechanization alone has acted as *the* god of ecocide. Rather, the interweaving of these forces in collusion one with the other has shaped our heritage and bequeathed to us the multifaceted dilemmas we now face. Patriarchy's hierarchy of values and category of otherness supported Christianity's devaluing of the unredeemable and disvaluing of the material earth. Christian dominion-over complemented patriarchy's objectification and mechanism's utilitarianism. Christian dominion-over facilitated mechanistic mastery and patriarchal domination while Christian stewardship facilitated scientific and mechanistic management (and exploitation) of resources. The imperialistic thrust of Christianity sanctioned patriarchal control and helped to spread the gospel of the god of the machine. Neither patriarchy, Christianity, nor mechanism has valued the earth for its own sake as something intrinsically worth caring for and about in its own right. And patriarchy's urge toward transcendence, Christianity's other-worldliness, and mechanistic science's theoretical technology have functioned together to completely disvalue both this life and this earth. It has indeed been a complex process with far from satisfactory results. And yet, we are not called to give up hope, to despair, or to bury a dying planet. Our ecotheological deconstructions instead invite us to attempt healing and restorative reconstructions, to create new visions for a whole living earth. Feminist and gay liberation theology already bear the seeds of liberation that can enable us to shape a gay ecotheology that holds forth the promise of the renewal and rebirth of our earth, our home. That is the task that still invitingly awaits us.

Gaia and the Healing of Theology and Nature

It's rather significant, we think, that those who have no compassion have no wisdom. Knowledge, yes; cleverness, maybe; wisdom, no. A clever mind is not a heart. Knowledge doesn't really care. Wisdom does.
—Benjamin Hoff, *The Tao of Pooh*

God/ess-with-Us:
An Immanent and Interdependent Relation

One of the various approaches to the process of healing the earth begins with healing human consciousness insofar as humanity acts as the clearest threat to the biosphere. One way to heal our consciousness is to reconstruct theology, to create new visions and new understandings that dispel the villainous confluence of heteropatriarchy, imperialist Christianity, and divinized mechanism. One way to do this begins with reconsidering the divine itself. Traditional Christianity, for example, has required belief in a male ruler god, an idolatrous image of male sovereignty and domination. Moreover, our subservience to this god has required that we reject any attachment to the earth or to this life in favor of a transcendent, eschatological, or otherworldly spirituality. As we have already seen, such religiously grounded domination and otherworldliness have led to the exploitation and expendability of peoples and the earth. As gay men and lesbians, our experience of oppression, exclusion,

47

and expendability, as well as our experience of god/ess' companionship and empowerment radically intimate among us, leads us to be highly critical of these traditional, oppressive, and ecologically destructive motifs in theology. We recognize with Anne Primavesi that because both Judaism and Christianity have placed too much emphasis on "verbal sources," both oral and written, as the vehicles of a purely vertical revelation from on high, this two-pronged religious tradition has essentially failed to see god/ess present in and through all things, especially in nonhuman nature or in things earthly and earthy, like sexuality.[1] Our experience as *the* authoritative resource for our theology and our ecotheology contravenes this history of vertical, transcendent revelation and insists instead upon the radical horizontality or immanence of the divine in and through all of life here and now.

This conflation of the divine with biospheric life and experience also conflates the dualism of god-above/earth-below. Without this ultimate dualism, the oppressive and exploitative power of all the other dualisms should also dissipate. To heal our theology, our visions, and the earth, we must in fact dispense with all dualisms and the hierarchical values they entail, especially the separations of sacred and profane, of transcendence and immanence, and of spirit and matter. The bottom line is that a radically horizontal god/ess-with-us is immanent or incarnate in everything, throughout all life in both biosphere and geosphere. Ultimately, matter and spirit are one; all is sacred. The divine cosmic energy is interwoven into and interspersed throughout our very lives, our physical embodiments, and everything that constitutes life, earth, and cosmos. Or, as Brian Swimme has noted, "This creative interlacing energy envelopes us entirely."[2]

Explicated in detail in that gay liberation theology that is shaped by feminist paradigms[3] and absolutely important for a gay ecotheology that extends the efforts of ecofeminism, a radically horizontal and intimate god/ess interspersed among all things, one interdependent and cosuffering with all creation, is not really transcendent at all but is utterly immanent, absolutely part and parcel of this world, this life, this earth, this cosmos. The transcendence/ immanence dualism dissipates because transcendence is revealed as an empty concept, an illusion. As such, god/ess in godself demands our respectful caring not only for one another, humanly speaking, but for all the earth as well—for all its peoples, for all its nonhuman life in the biosphere, and for the geophysical life of the planet itself as an ever developing and changing organism. Weather, earthquakes, volcanoes, plate tectonics—all testify that the earth, as geosphere, is just as alive in its own way, as is the earth as biosphere. We are a part of both together and so is the divine.

This liberational understanding of the divine as intimately alongside all that is has been given its most thorough articulation in the work of Alfred North Whitehead and other process theologians.[4] More recently, process theology, or panentheism, has been given fresh voice by various feminist writers. A monotheistic, panentheistic theology, such as any of these, sees god/ess as both physical and spiritual energy. As energy, the physical and the spiritual are no longer dualistic opposites but are conflated, one. God/ess includes all that is, but the divine is not limited to the sum of the parts. Sallie McFague, for example, describes panentheism as "a view of the God-world relationship in which all things have their origins in God and nothing exists outside God, though this does not mean that God is reduced to those things."[5] McFague goes on to create a related image of the divine that she hopes will facilitate both an appreciation of divine immanence and the assumption of human responsibility for ecological healing. She argues that, in the traditional patriarchal view, "God can be god only if we are nothing" and that "God is worldless and the world is godless: the world is empty of God's presence." The traditional model of the divine "encourages a sense of distance from the world; it attends only to the human dimension of the world; and, it supports attitudes of either domination of the world or passivity toward it."[6] Because traditional, hierarchical Christian theology has fostered, at best, an absence of concern for the earth and, at worst, the full exploitation of the earth, McFague recommends envisioning the divine not as over above the earth, but as the earth. For her, envisioning "the world as God's body" radically underscores "the intimacy of God and creation" in a way vastly different from the traditional, hierarchical view of the world as dominated by a god who is above and distant from the world.[7]

More recently, Nancy Howell has poignantly extended McFague's metaphor in a way that powerfully underscores the divine's caring intimacy: "Pregnant with the world, God's experience is consumed with the demands, the movements, the distresses, and the passions of the world to which God responds in God's body," that is to say, the very world itself.[8] Clearly, then, we can understand the divine in such a way that god/ess is no longer viewed as vertically alien and transcendent; instead, god/ess may be understood as a radically horizontal and intimately near companion and co-creator, one interwoven into the very fabric of all that is. As such, god/ess truly "delights in the creation and suffers wherever it is destroyed."[9]

The image of "the world as God's body" has an immediate resonance with gay liberation theology and, through that resonance, clear implications for ecological concern. Ron Long has insisted that "we are our bodies"; we cannot know or experience life apart from our embodied states in this life.[10] God/ess' own embodiment as earth-world-cosmos takes this notion a further step. Just as we cannot experience life apart from our embodied life on earth—in these bodies we now have, despite their physical and mortal limitations, and despite whatever problems those limitations may present for theology[11]—neither can we experience life apart from *this* earth, *this* biosphere, *this* geosphere. If indeed our science fiction is whimsy at best and transcendent escapism at worst, we must instead affirm the earth as our dearly valued and necessary home;[12] if the time ever does come when technology allows us to visit other planets, we will bear no less responsibility for the integrity of those planets and their inhabitants and we will still need to honor the earth as that home that nurtures our going forth and that welcomes our return. We cannot live apart from the earth and its larger home, this universe and this cosmos, which, as the full embodiment of the divine, also demand our loving respect and care.

We should, however, be very cautious about the hubris and utilitarianism implicit here. The earth is not the embodiment of god/ess merely for our egotistical pursuits or needs. Indeed, when Charlene Spretnak argues that "what was cosmologically wholesome and healing was the discovery of the divine as immanent in and around us,"[13] she is implying that realizing such radical immanence—god/ess *so* near, embodied in sunrises, trees and flowers, sea otters and seals, oceans and forests, embodied every bit as much in nonhuman nature as in people—utterly contradicts the human arrogance in the assumption that only people are created in the divine image, *imago dei*. Radical immanence offers a spiritual alternative to such theological hubris: "Extremely important is a willingness to deepen our experience of communion with nature. This can be done in the mountains, at the ocean, in a city park, or a backyard garden."[14] One resonance for urbanized gay men in particular is that sunbathing, bicycling, exercising and body building, even the body sweat of dancing—once we get past the enculturated sexual subtexts in these experiences and learn to embrace them and to value them as ends in themselves—these begin to open us to experience the cosmically embodied, earthly embodied immanence of the divine in all things, not just in humanity. Indeed, the realization that divine immanence is not just about human creation *imago dei* or about the earth's utilitarian value as the human home further enables us to see that immanence is not about human dependence and exploitation but is rather about the interdependence and interconnectedness of all that is. Only in learning these concepts do we truly begin to appreciate the meaning of ecological communion.

Because human nature is inherently egocentric, the best way into an appreciation of the interdependence of all that is might appear to be from our human point of view. Rosemary Radford Ruether, for example, anticipates my affirmation that we cannot live apart from the earth and uses that anthropocentric vantage point in a way that should enable us to begin to value the importance of our interdependence. She says, "The more complex forms of life . . . are radically dependent on all the stages of life that go before them and that continue to underlie their own existence. . . . Human beings cannot live without the whole ecological community that supports and makes possible our existence."[15] However, Ruether also astutely realizes that such a naive egocentrism may not be enough to motivate change. The philosophical concept of "enlightened self-interest" can be understood to mean that egocentric human beings often have to be reminded of threats to their egocentric position before they actually get motivated. Waiting until humans perceive themselves as threatened ecologically, while people continue to violate the interdependence of all that is, takes just that risk. Consequently, Ruether also pessimistically expects that ultimately "the universe will create inversions, under the weight of human distortion and oppression, that will undermine the whole human life-support system. . . . We may . . . bring the earth down with us in our downfall"; consequently, "we cannot violate the ecological community without ultimately destroying our own life-support system."[16] Anne Primavesi reiterates Ruether's warning when she adds, "Nature is through and through relational, and interference at one point has interminable and unforeseen effects."[17] More to the point, James Nash echoes Ruether's frustration when he recognizes the damage already caused by our humanly egocentric refusal to acknowledge our cosmic interdependence. He notes, for example, that human "assumptions of isolation and fragmentation . . . have [already] caused ecological disasters by neglecting relationships—for instance, the connections between ozone depletion and CFCs, global warming and the burning of fossil fuels, population growth and resource depletion, or habitat destruction and species' extinction."[18]

Ruether's pessimism and Nash's assessment of damages already accrued make it clear that human egocentrism has myopically failed to acknowledge our interdependence and has precluded our acting responsibly. Our patriarchal and hierarchical sense of self-importance has left us alienated from our home, this earth that we insist on exploiting, as Carol Christ elaborates:

> *We have lost the sense that this earth is our home, and we fail to recognize our profound connection with all beings in the web of life. Instead, many people uncritically accept the view that "man" is superior to "nature" and has the right to "use" the natural world in any way "he" sees fit. . . . [In contrast,] the preservation of the earth requires . . . a recovery of more ancient and traditional views that revere the profound connection of all beings in the web of life.* [19]

Our efforts to recover "more ancient and traditional" views hold the liberating potential to shatter our myopic vision. When our eyes are ecologically and liberationally opened, we come to realize that such a healing view once permeated the very lands that we have imperialistically inherited. Those of us who are the descendants of the Euro-American intruders on this continent must be careful not to coopt Native American wisdom as if it represented our own insights. That is just another form of imperialism. Nevertheless, we should realize that many of those Native Americans, whose lives our ancestors found expendable and whose lands they found exploitable, understood the interdependent and relational aspects of their position within nature. As a native of the southern Appalachians and a resident of north central Georgia, I am especially embarrassed and angered, for example, by the ways in which the intruding Euro-Americans of this region treated the Cherokees, and I am also deeply appreciative of the wisdom entailed in the Cherokee's "concept of natural balance":

> *While the industrialized nations have for so long assumed that nature exists for [people] to use in any way [they] see fit, and that nature is infinitely forgiving, the Cherokees recognized that [people] had to exploit nature in order to live, but that [people] should do so carefully, and that nature was not infinitely forgiving. If mistreated, nature could strike back. . . . The Cherokees realized that [humanity] tends to abuse*

nature, and that [people] can become too populous, and that when [they do,] nature suffers. . . . Their concept of natural balance would seem to have a long-term superiority over our own. [20]

This historical wisdom has recently been reiterated by Osage/ Cherokee writer George Tinker. Countering Euro-American individualism and consumerism, he reminds us that we humans are part of a greater whole within which the values of respect and reciprocity are the most ecologically sound. Respect as an ecological value helps to "maintain the harmony and balance, the interdependence and interrelationship of all things in our world"; reciprocity is the concerted effort to give something "back to the earth and to all of Creation in order to maintain balance even as we disrupt the balance" in seeking food, creating shelter, and meeting other basic needs. [21]

What the recovered wisdom of "more ancient and traditional views" is trying to tell us is that "the earth is alive, part of a living cosmos," and that, as a living organism, the earth requires our empathy in relationship, as Starhawk notes when she says, "When we start to understand that the earth is alive, she calls us to act to preserve her life." [22] In fact, valuing the interdependence of all things is not likely to spring from human egocentrism; rather, recognizing our fundamental interconnectedness in the web of being may serve as the requisite antidote to our human hubris. Both gay liberation theology and our developing ecotheology prophetically remind us that living and being in relation—our fundamental relationality, interconnectedness, or interdependence—includes being in relation to all other peoples, especially all other oppressed peoples, and, most important in the present context, it also entails being in relation to the earth, to all life and life processes human and non-human, plant and animal, and processes meteorological and geophysical. I want to affirm with Carol Christ that "I imagine that all that is cares" and that "we do not need to know that our moral will is in the image of a personal god/ess in order to know that we have the capacity to create death or to love and preserve life"; instead of the egocentrism of a human *imago dei* in ecological ethics or elsewhere, what we need is "an ethic rooted in a desire to enhance the life possibilities of all beings, both human and nonhuman."[23]

Our ecological ethics of interdependence and interconnectedness will not only acknowledge and honor "the embeddedness of all the earth's peoples in the multiple webs and cycles of life,"[24] but will go even further, taking "heed of the intricate webs that link the birth and well-being of all animals, human as well as nonhuman, with the well-being of the earth's ecosystems.[25] After all, as Catherine Keller has reminded us, "We are, as is everything that is, an instance of becoming-in-relation. Nothing is independent of anything else. This is the fundamental ecological vision, applicable to human culture as well as to nonhuman communities."[26] This fundamental reality of interdependence and interconnectedness, of becoming-in-relation, means we can no longer accept any hierarchical evaluation of human over nonhuman, animal over plant, biosphere over geosphere. Because "we are part of an immense complexity of subtly balanced relationships" whereby human and nonhuman, plants and animals, biosphere and geosphere are delicately and intimately interwoven, not only must we "accept intellectually the interactive nature of our own and other ecosystems," but we must also learn to behave "in a way which fosters a healthy interaction between organism, society, and the world."[27]

Just as god/ess and world are immanently and intimately interwoven and interdependent as one, so too the intimately interwoven and immensely complex interdependent relationality of all that is suggests that we are again describing oneness, the pluriformity-in-one of an ecological system. Or, as Primavesi reminds us, "An ecological paradigm demands that we cultivate a sense of belonging to a system that functions as a whole. . . . Then it demands that we extend our awareness to the other systems with which we interact and their interactions with further ones."[28] These complexes of systems in relational interaction constitute the larger organic system that is life itself and that, as such, is also god/ess-with-us. In so acknowledging the ubiquity of both the divine and nature, or life, in and through all our being and all our fundamentally interdependent and relational interactions, we move away from human *egocentrism* toward *ecocentrism*, an ecologically sound self-understanding and spirituality that affirms that all is One.

Clearly the move from egocentrism to ecocentrism means that we finally realize that "the human and the earth are totally implicated each in the other."[29] This "implication" of absolute interconnectedness also has further implications for our spirituality and our ecotheology. Thomas Berry, for example, insists that we need to (re)learn to recognize the "numinous qualities of the earth"; to recover in the process our "capacity for subjective communion with the earth [and for] identification with the cosmic-earth-human process"; and ultimately to develop and nurture "a spirituality that emerges out of a reality deeper than ourselves, even deeper than life, a spirituality that is as deep as . . . the entire cosmic-earth process."[30]

Resonances of this ecocentric spirituality already reverberate throughout both feminist and gay liberation theology. First of all, we are reminded of the fundamental ways in which our sexuality at its best is an urging into relationship with another person and, implicitly through that relationship, also an urging for justice in all relationships, including our relationship with the earth itself. This erotic connectedness running throughout these theologies is articulately summarized by Primavesi when she writes, "Sexuality sensitizes the entire body to respond to all other forms of life in the world—person, animal, flower, or river."[31]

Second, an ecocentric conflation of vertical hierarchies into a radically horizontal and divinely immanent whole, or system, or web of interdependent and interconnected relations further means that power-over is no longer a reasonable understanding of power. We do not need or desire any dominating power in our lives or over the earth. What we do need is to recognize and (re)value the power from within the earth that is already present "as connectedness, sustenance, healing, creating." According to Primavesi, such earthly power "enables us to exercise power-with . . . to cooperate, to share, to change. . . . This is a caring [and relational] form of power."[32] Power-with is the empowerment of god/ess-with-us that lies at the heart of feminist and gay liberation theology and of ecofeminism and our gay ecotheology.

Finally, an ecocentric spirituality transforms our values as we experience hierarchically exclusive values "transvalued" into an all-inclusive valuing of the integrity and liberation of all life. Writes Carol Christ, "To understand and value the life we enjoy is to understand and value the lives of all other beings, human and nonhuman. . . . We begin to understand that it is a violation of the web of life to take more than we need."[33] Perhaps the most important result of this transvaluation of values is the opening up toward all-inclusiveness that this enables; valuing inclusivity enables us at last to revalue, reappreciate, and celebrate the rich diversity of all that is. The hope that connects gay ecotheology with gay liberation theology is the belief that if people can learn to value diversity throughout all life, then they will also appreciate diversity in human life. Then homophobia will disappear; then no one and no thing will ever be expendable again. Summarizes Christ, "In addition to inspiring respect for all beings in the web of life, the vision of connection encourages greater appreciation for the diversity of human experience."[34]

DIVERSITY: A CELEBRATION OF INTRINSIC VALUING

Inevitably, the value hierarchies that have resulted from the dualisms of heteropatriarchy have also led large numbers of people mistakenly to assume that "from the point of view of the 'higher,' difference automatically implies inferiority."[35] In their efforts to correct this mistaken assumption and to reaffirm the value of difference, feminist theologians have long argued that we need to "reestablish our sense of ecological wholeness, of diversity in unity" and that we need to revalue the concepts of care, reciprocity, and diversity so that "our sense of oneness with nature" is thoroughly connected "with concrete loving actions."[36] True communion with divinely immanent life itself thus eschews transcendence and becomes restorative praxis. The grounding for these feminist theological correctives once again is not some patriarchal authority but lies rather in the resonating authority of women's experience for doing theology and builds upon the concepts of oneness and interdependence discussed earlier. From her Whiteheadian perspective, for example, Nancy Howell argues that because god/ess and the world are so interdependent, "diversity in the world is the primary contributor to [god/ess'] rich experience"; in other words, "ecological diversity contributes first to prospects for survival of the biosphere and then fosters potential for rich experience in the biospheric future."[37] More straightforward than Howell in drawing upon the authority of experience, Primavesi simply asserts, "The fact that creation contains the infinite variety that it obviously does contain... leads to the conclusion that [god/ess] has a preference for diversity."[38]

Marti Kheel also draws upon authoritative experience, affirming oneness and the interconnectedness of diversity, while also leading us to an important qualifying caveat. She says, "Our deep holistic awareness of the interconnectedness of all of life must be a *lived* awareness that we experience in relation to *particular* beings *as well as* the larger whole."[39] In other words, because the transcendent tendency in patriarchy too often devalues particulars, a healthy appreciation of the oneness of the earth, the cosmos, and all things must not preclude attention to and appreciation of the rich diversity of particular individuals, both human and nonhuman. Our caring must be directed toward particular individual persons, animals, plants, species, and so on, as well as toward the whole. This is the meaning of pluriformity-in-one. As Kheel herself says, "The danger of an abstract identification with a larger 'whole' is that it fails to recognize or respect the existence of independent, living beings"; it also reflects the patriarchal mindset, seeking "to transcend the concrete world of particularity in preference for something more enduring and abstract."[40]

Feminist theologians are not alone either in demonstrating

patriarchy's disdain for diversity or in seeking to revalue diversity and the richness of pluriform interrelatedness. In fact, because ecofeminist analysis examines these issues only in reference to patriarchy's exploitation of those things and people categorized as different, as "other," that analysis does not go far enough. The value of diversity and difference, however, may be *the* significant leitmotif of a gay ecotheology that functions as a broader analysis than ecofeminism—as a larger, intellectual concentric circle, if you will, that most certainly includes ecofeminism within its own larger inclusivity. Gay ecotheology, therefore, focuses not only upon patriarchy's exploitation of, but more critically still upon *hetero*-patriarchy's attitudes of expendability toward, those things and people categorized as different, as "other." Within our present heterosexist culture, gay men and lesbians are *the* paradigmatically different "other" whose experiences of utter disvaluation and exclusion, of homophobia and antigay/lesbian violence, including violent hate-motivated murder, and of victim-blaming and medical neglect during the AIDS health crisis, altogether shape our authoritative voice, our righteously angry and defiant scream that demands the revaluation of diversity, of pluriformity. Because we who are gay men and lesbians realize all too well the extent to which heteropatriarchy's attitudes of expendability undergird and encourage antigay/lesbian "homo-cide," we also fully realize that, ecologically speaking, the "failure to preserve the diversity of interdependent beings is ecocidal."[41]

Our differences and our expendability, both literally and metaphorically, stand prophetically over against heteropatriarchy's ecologically disastrous attitudes of planned obsolescence and disposable goods. We will not be thrown away. Nor can we allow our society to dispose of the earth. Painfully, and all too often, ecofeminist analysis stops just short of such radical inclusivity. Again, as an example, Catherine Keller writes, "To honor reality is to attend carefully to the diversity of each moment"; we need "a new understanding of human socioecology—one that cherishes our own diversity rather than exploiting it through hierarchies of state, race, class, and gender."[42] Where is sexual orientation in such an analysis? Must gay men and lesbians remain invisible—already excluded, disposed of, predisposed against? Our gay ecotheology defiantly shouts a resounding "No" to that exclusion. We assume the authority to rewrite that analysis, affirming that we need more; we need in fact to cherish our own diversity rather than disposing of it through hierarchies of state, race, class, gender, *and sexual orientation*. We will not remain invisible, disvalued, discounted, disposed. The diversity of the earth will not remain invisible either. We will defiantly celebrate the value of our difference as well as the rich diversity of all that is.

A potential caveat also seeps through our analysis, however, as it did for our feminist colleague Marti Kheel. There are dangers in arguing either that "we are just the same as" some other minority or even nongay people or that "we are different from" whomever. The former makes us ripe for cooptation by the forces of assimilation and oppression and can lead to our being identified with the oppressor. The latter, however, risks reinforcing the rationale by which the oppressor brackets and disvalues us. As a people, we need to learn to acknowledge and celebrate both the commonalities and the diversity among ourselves without also creating exclusive value/disvalue hierarchies based on our own diversity. We must also extend our vision beyond the ghetto of in-group needs and agendas, however necessary and urgent they may be, to see and to make the connections between our experience of oppression and that of others, as well as between our own sense of difference and the importance of diversity throughout the whole earth. As we cooperatively seek the liberation and healing of all peoples and the earth, our own in-group needs and agendas will be fulfilled and our own liberation accomplished along the way. Indeed, gay ecotheology's critique of ecofeminism, for example, is offered not as a competitive, patriarchal assault, but rather as a contribution to creative dialogue that facilitates a liaison by which we extend the elegant and painstakingly thorough scholarship that our feminist colleagues had undertaken long before we discovered our own capacity to join

them in seeking our mutual liberation and empowerment. In celebrating our difference and in claiming the value of diversity, we are
in essence insisting not only that gay men and lesbians have intrinsic value, a priori, but that all the earth, all life, also has *intrinsic*
value.

Part of the joint task of ecofeminism and gay ecotheology is to
radically affirm that earth, life, and nature—biosphere and geosphere—are absolutely intrinsically valuable. We must go beyond
the management-stewardship mentality and its mere conservation
of utilitarian, instrumentally valued "natural resources," whether
human or nonhuman, biological or geological, to acknowledge not
only our utter interdependence and interconnectedness with the
full web of life but also the absolute value of all that is. Our reverence for life must become reverence for being itself, for all that is,
as we extend the power of the verb "to be" to the extent that we include all the biosphere and all the geosphere within the sphere of
being, which is god/ess-immanently-with-us.[43] In acknowledging
the interdependence of all things, Carolyn Merchant has said that
"the environment prescribes human behavior and its limits, since
exploitation will ultimately lead to extinction [for *all* life]. Environmental ethics is thus not merely an ethic about the environment but an ethic determined by it as well."[44] In a similar vein,
Nancy Howell has argued that any instrumental value in an ecological perspective derives not from any hierarchy, but rather from our
utter interdependence; therefore, instrumental value should not be
hierarchicalized or viewed anthropomorphically.[45]

An ethic determined by the environment, however, should
move beyond even the implicit utilitarian value that Merchant and
Howell, like Ruether earlier, still unwittingly assign to nature. If
we do not assume that humanity's long-term survival is any more
valuable than the long-term survival of any other life form (divinely, cosmically, or even evolutionarily speaking), and if we do
not risk reducing the biosphere to just the life-support system for a
still hierarchically valued humanity, only then do we achieve an
understanding of all diversity and all life as genuinely intrinsically

valuable. Such radically nonhierarchical, intrinsic valuation again brings us into the sphere of Native American wisdom. According to George Tinker, the Native American view does not give a hierarchical priority to the human. People, nature, and divine are "coequal participants in the circle [of creation], standing neither above nor below anything else. . . . There is no hierarchy . . . even of species, because the circle has no beginning nor ending. Hence all the createds participate together, each in their own way, to preserve the wholeness of the circle."[46] In other words, we humans are related to, kin with, all of creation; we humans are not inherently better than or more valuable than any other life. There is intrinsic value or inherent worth in all of life. Consequently, we need to nurture within ourselves the capacity to "experience evil or sin as disruptions in that delicate balance, disruptions that negate the intrinsic worth of any of our relatives."[47]

Tinker's use of traditional terminology such as "evil or sin" easily facilitates connecting his particular expression of Native American wisdom with similar ecofeminist insights. In terms reminiscent of Sallie McFague, Anne Primavesi makes just such a connection: "To celebrate the living body of earth is to celebrate it as it is in itself. . . . Each being has a value that is inherent, that cannot be diminished, rated, or ranked, that does not have to be earned or granted. . . . Nature not only has its own relationships, its own innate values, but also its intrinsic rights [such as] the 'rights' of wild places to exist *for their own sake*."[48] Speaking more traditionally still, divinely immanent grace permeates the entire web of being, not just human being. In Whiteheadian terms Nancy Howell similarly insists that "humans are continuous with the rest of nature as an integral part of the natural process," a continuity without any hierarchy of values, which is reaffirmed by Whitehead's belief in the "pervasive subjectivity in *all* entities. . . . Whiteheadians argue that both organic and inorganic entities are experiencing creatures" and thus that all are equally valuable a priori.[49] Within the Whiteheadian "organic matrix of nature," god/ess' intentions, or the most realistic best possibilities in every instance, are offered equally to all the earth, to human and nonhuman, to biosphere and geosphere alike.[50]

Even James Nash at first appears to join these celebrations of intrinsic value when he says that we need "to save other creatures for their sake, not solely for the sake of humanity."[51] But, as noted earlier, Nash soon contradicts himself with a hierarchy of values that betrays his actual "speciesism"—an anthropocentric and egocentric placement "of the human species at the center of one's attention."[52] And, of course, Nash later freely admits that the world has only "an interim goodness";[53] he grants this world only a penultimate goodness, a value still to be superseded by the "next" world, and not a final or intrinsic goodness in and of itself. He is ultimately quite arrogant in his unquestioning assumption of hierarchical values that trivializes any nonhierarchical alternative. He writes, for example, "Nearly all of us act routinely on hierarchical assumptions in our daily lives, like swatting flies."[54] In contrast, our ecotheology must insist that while we may necessarily act in a graded or hierarchical manner—against certain insects or health-endangering microorganisms, or simply as predators in the food chain—nevertheless, these self-preferring actions should not be taken to imply that any other organism is inherently less valuable in the cosmic scheme of things. To assume, as Nash does, that humans are the unsurpassable pinnacle of creation is patriarchal Christian hubris of the worst kind.

Fortunately for both our theology and our ecology, it is possible to move away from both such hierarchical and egocentric values and such speciesism and back instead to "more holistic, less sequential thinking" that enables us again to "attend to our place in the whole." According to Martha Ellen Stortz, there is in fact a conceivable "moral universe that could include things human and things not human: nature, the environment, the ecosphere, animals, the solar system, the cosmos—mysterious and complex as that notion is."[55] Not dissimilarly, Sallie McFague tries to achieve some middle ground, albeit far from Nash, as she weaves between the implicit preferential treatment still allowed humanity by Mer-

chant and Howell and the unabashed affirmation of absolute intrinsic value in Tinker, Primavesi, and Stortz. True to her metaphor, she concludes that "the world is a body that must be carefully
tended, that must be nurtured, protected, guided, loved, and be-
friended *both* as valuable in itself—for like us, it is an expression of
[god/ess]—and as necessary to the continuation of life."[56]

Virtually nowhere is the prophetic mandate of such wisdom
more clear than in regard to minority and third-world peoples.
Apart from the expendability meted out to gay men and lesbians in
our own country, nothing else so testifies to the exploitative and
disposing mentality of the (hetero)patriarchy or so clearly witnesses
for the need to reappreciate the intrinsic value of difference and diversity among peoples and the earth. For example, in order to find
a reasonable and affordable home, my spouse and I live in what is
euphemistically termed a "transitional," older neighborhood on
the south side of Atlanta. Although some portions of the neighborhood (several blocks west of us) have been "gentrified" and restored, the majority of the neighborhood is still African American
and Hispanic as a result of the "white flight" to the eastern suburbs
that occurred in the 1960s. Over the last several decades the neighborhood was hemmed in by now abandoned industries—an empty
warehouse complex not too far south of us, an automobile assembly
plant to the southwest that fell victim to the economy—as well as
by the baseball stadium and its leveled blocks of parking to the west
and by the CSX piggyback rail facility and an abandoned cotton
and bag mill to the northeast. Thirty years ago, the northernmost
part of the neighborhood was severed by the east expressway and an
additional barrier to the more affluent (white) northern side of the
city was later created by the rapid transit line that parallels that expressway. Now, despite concerted restoration progress, the large
city park that houses the city's zoo and civil war memorial, and cooperative, interracial neighborhood activism, because the neighborhood is still perceived as only a south side, African American
neighborhood, we cannot even attract a major grocery store or

drugstore to serve our immediate community. We spend entirely too much time in our cars getting basic necessities.

A similar example is my grandmother's much smaller southern town. She still lives in a house that lies in what is increasingly becoming a no-person's-land in the heart of the town. She is between what her generation still calls the "colored college" and a "downtown" of a half-dozen blocks of virtually empty and/or abandoned stores whose merchants have fled to the outlying strip malls. In her neighborhood, as houses like the one next door burn, they sit until they collapse and the city finally clears them away; none are ever rebuilt. The city's abandoned and partially collapsed swimming pool complex a few blocks east has collected junked cars and trucks for years. In a once thriving neighborhood where people walked to church and to "town," my grandmother can now see across the emptied, overgrown lots to the wrecked, no doubt oil-dripping and polluting cars, and beyond to the college, and she has so many locks on her doors that coming or going is always a major ordeal. These two examples in my own experience are illustrations of a generalized situation that ecofeminist Cynthia Hamilton has described:

> *Minority communities shoulder a disproportionately high share of the by-products of industrial development: waste, abandoned factories and warehouses [and homes and vehicles], leftover chemicals and debris. These communities are also asked to house the waste and pollution no longer acceptable in white communities, such as hazardous landfills or dump sites.* [57]

She cites as a further example Los Angeles' intention to build a "13-acre incinerator...burning 2,000 tons a day of municipal waste...in a poor residential, Black, and Hispanic community," a project that neighborhood women, primarily, were eventually able to stop.[58]

The same patriarchal attitudes that devalue minority peoples and their neighborhoods in our own country and that further promote using those neighborhoods as the locations for society's disposable goods and expendable people, such as the homeless, are also the same attitudes that an imperialistic patriarchy has foisted upon much of the rest of the world. The devaluation and disvaluation of people of color has been extended to the Third World, whose peoples and lands are consistently treated as "resources" to exploit and expend. Susan Griffin makes these connections clearer when she says, "Disregard for the natural ecology of a region goes hand in hand with a disregard for the natural rights of people to determine their own fate and to live in the way they choose. This pattern of domination and disregard has created many of the famines in Africa."[59]

The most articulate ecofeminist voice to speak to this issue of the patriarchal abuse of third-world peoples and environments is that of Vandana Shiva. She notes, for example, that "the western development model... has become a source of the deprivation of basic needs" in third-world countries and she describes the "increasing scarcity of water, food, fodder, and fuel associated with... the ecological destruction" wreaked by development.[60] She is especially critical of the Western development mindset that superimposes its exploitative, consumerist values and actions on other people. This mentality sees no value in simpler, less exploitative, subsistence-based life-styles; it does not appreciate cultural diversity and consequently uses its power-over to compel third-world peoples to want and to achieve commodity-based life-styles similar to our own. The ecological consequences have been disastrous. These interconnected concerns, summarized in Shiva's cryptic comment that "more commodities and more cash mean less life— in nature through ecological destruction and in society through a denial of basic needs,"[61] are given elegant expression throughout her essay:

> *The linear reductionist view superimposes the roles and forms of power of the western male on women, all non-western peoples, and even on nature. Based on these... values and concepts, nature,*

women, and indigenous third world peoples become "deficient," in need of development. Diversity—and the unity and harmony in diversity—become epistemologically unattainable. . . .

The paradox and crises of development arise from the mistaken identification of culturally perceived poverty [commodity values] as real material poverty [subsistence values] and the mistaken identification of the growth of commodity production as solving basic needs. But the growing ecological crises and the ecological roots of poverty and the threat to survival indicate that . . . there is less water, less fertile soil, less genetic wealth as a result of the development process.[62]

Third-world peoples, however, are not standing passively by while Western patriarchy rapes their lands and invalidates their cultural values. They are realizing their own intrinsic value and the importance of their difference as enriching the diversity of the earth and in so doing they are discovering the immanent empowerment to resist patriarchal development and destruction. The most celebrated example of this empowerment in the ecological literature is that of the *Chipko andolan*, or tree-hugging movement, in India. When some three hundred ash trees were allotted to a sporting goods manufacturer by local forest officials in March 1973, villagers, again primarily women, literally hugged the trees to protect them from removal by the developers. The villagers had perceived the connections between constant tree felling in their region, extensive soil erosion, and severe flooding that had occurred in 1970 and again in 1973. Not only did the tree-hugging process succeed this time, but it was used effectively again in other areas in 1977 and 1980.[63] Even here in Atlanta, a similar process has been used, as people climbed into the trees and chained themselves to the trees that lay in the path of yet another planned eastern expressway that would have plowed through several transitional neighborhoods. After nearly two decades of protests by a coalition of neighborhoods, the road has not been extended to its originally planned length; it has, however, been approved through the poorest, largely

African American, residential neighborhood that lies closest to downtown—a sad patriarchal reality that would not surprise Hamilton, Griffin, or Shiva.

While the patriarchal mentality still trashes and paves over minority neighborhoods, still strips the rainforests bare, still harms certain wildlife and habitats to near extinction in pursuit of development and commodities—use and abuse—people *are* resisting. Change *is* occurring. Just like gay men and lesbians, people everywhere are beginning to realize and to claim their own intrinsic value and to celebrate their own difference and the larger diversity that their difference enriches. As the disempowered peoples of the earth come to appreciate the intrinsic value and diversity of the human community, *those* values will be superimposed upon nature, supplanting the patriarchal values superimposed upon nature until now. Healing, caring, and nurturing will increasingly supplant exploiting and disposing of nature. These processes may have only begun, but they are nonetheless already reshaping both ecology and theology in liberational and restorative ways.

Ecotheologisms

The processes of deconstructing the multifaceted specter of heteropatriarchy, of reconstructing a radically immanent and interdependent understanding of the divine-world-human nexus of interrelationships, and, thereby, of realizing the intrinsic value of all that is and thus revaluing cosmic, earthly, and even human diversity further enables us to look with fresh eyes at certain traditional religious concepts. Our developing gay ecotheological perspective will disclose liberating and ecologically sound ways to revision these concepts as well.

"Sin and Judgment"

Traditionally, for example, the concept of sin has most frequently been reduced to the context of privatized sexual *acts*; we have been far more interested, and pruriently so, in the sexual behavior of human individuals than in the systemic or structural foundations of oppression, exploitation, and expendability. As feminist and gay liberation theologies have already seen, our culture has focused on sinful *acts* rather than on the fundamentally sinful condition that undergirds heteropatriarchy itself.[64] In the present context, James Nash similarly contends, "Sin too often has been functionally limited . . . to sexual misdeeds. . . . In our own time . . . the meaning of sin must be properly extended to cover ecological misdeeds and the human condition underlying them."[65] Clearly, an ecologically sound understanding of "sin" will focus not upon sexual acts, but rather upon the choices human beings make within their own ecosystem(s) in interdependent relation to other creatures and to god/ess. We realize that rejecting one's fellow creatures on the earth, both plants and animals in the biosphere as well as the geosphere itself, and rejecting one's responsibility toward all things within the interconnected web of being constitute sinful behavior. Or, as Sallie McFague has said, "To sin is . . . to refuse to take responsibility for nurturing, loving, and befriending the body and all its parts. Sin is the refusal to realize one's radical interdependence with all that lives; it is the desire to set oneself apart from all others as not needing them or being needed by them."[66] Sin is the willful disruption of our kinship, of our fundamental interrelationship with all that is.[67]

The fundamental condition of sinfulness is something deeper than actions alone, whether sexual or ecological; the fundamental condition of sinfulness is the very anthropomorphism, human arrogance, or egocentrism that permeates our culture and society. Ecologically speaking, sin is the self-centered disregard for any other being that inevitably causes us to fail to act responsibly. It entails acting as if humans "owned" creation, while both overlooking natural limitations and disrespecting "the interdependent relationships of all creatures and their environments."[68] Or, as Anne Primavesi has said, "The creation and maintenance of structures . . . which are bound to block all effective forms of loving our fellow earth creatures [and that] prevent the recognition and growth of diversity [and that] foster an us-versus-them categorizing . . . remains the very essence of sin."[69]

Traditionally, the correlative of "sin" has been "judgment." However, within the context of liberationally and ecologically sound theology-as-praxis, we must be very careful whenever we impute judgment to any situation. Ecologically speaking, so-called natural disasters that are clearly traceable to human environmental abuses—whether the *Exxon Valdez*, or flooding caused by deforestation and soil erosion, or famines resulting from global warming—all carry within themselves their own "pedagogical judgment" that demands corrective human response in the present and for the future. Other natural disasters such as hurricanes, volcanoes, earthquakes, and so on, are value-neutral portions of the living earth's own necessary geospheric balancing and developing processes. *Neither* kind of natural occurrence should ever be interpreted in such a way as to attribute divine judgment upon certain groups of people or in any other way so as to "blame the victim."[70] Living in the age of AIDS, gay men in particular have become all too aware of the extent to which heteropatriarchy prefers to blame the victims of naturally occurring phenomena (such as the HIV virus) rather than to take responsibility for compassionate, corrective, and healing action in such crises. It is far easier to blame those who are different, those people and things categorized as "other," than to acknowledge the solidarity of cosuffering interconnectedness and to act accordingly. Our gay ecotheology resolutely refuses to condone such attitudes, eschews judgmentalism, and requires responsible right-relation instead toward all persons and toward the whole earth.

"Justice and Rights"

For gay men and lesbians, the connections we see between homophobia and AIDS-phobia directed toward us and that same attitude of disvaluation and expendability directed toward other peoples and the earth itself lead us to affirm that not judgment but justice as right-relation must be unfailingly sought in the human, the biospheric, and the geospheric arenas. As Carol Robb has stated, "We cannot escape having to argue for a new emphasis or a new priority in measures of justice in order to approach right relation" throughout the global community.[71] In fact, the connections we see between heteropatriarchy's disvaluation and disregard of gay/lesbian people and third-world peoples and its domination and exploitation of women and third-world environments have compelled us to realize that ecological justice must go hand in hand with social justice for *all* oppressed peoples and their environments. Starhawk is right when she adamantly insists that "environmental issues *are* social justice issues. . . . The ethics of integrity prevents us from accepting a solution for someone else that we are unwilling to accept for ourselves."[72] In other words, to seek justice as right-relation means that just as we cannot displace blame onto someone else, so neither can we shift responsibility onto someone else's shoulders. The interdependence of all things requires that *we* assume responsibility; the immanence of god/ess-with-us also requires that we assume responsibility because, as we do so, we empower godself to empower us in turn, for all our tasks of healing, both for people and the whole earth.

Rosemary Radford Ruether further elaborates these various connections:

> Any ecological ethic must always take into account the structures of social domination and exploitation that mediate domination of nature and prevent concern for the welfare of the whole [global] community in favor of the immediate advantage of the dominant class, race, and sex [and sexual orientation!]. An ecological ethic must always be an ethic of ecojustice that recognizes the interconnection of social domination and domination of nature.[73]

More recently, Dieter Hessel has pragmatically reiterated Ruether's concerns as he weaves together certain now familiar themes—ecojustice and social justice, diversity and intrinsic value. He also contends, for example, that we must attend to

> ecological integrity and social justice together. . . . [Ecojustice entails] constructive human responses that concentrate on the link between

ecological health and economic health. . . . Ecojustice occurs wherever human beings receive sufficient sustenance and build enough community to live harmoniously with [god/ess], each other, and all of nature [all its diversity], while they also appreciate the rest of creation for its own sake and not simply as useful to humanity.[74]

It becomes increasingly clear that, taken together, liberational concerns and ecotheological valuing enable the broadest possible perspective: human justice is included within/under ecojustice, gay/lesbian justice is included within/under human justice, and genuine peace flows out of/is made possible by justice, including economic and social justice. George Tinker, for example, approaches ecojustice as just this sort of umbrella concept. He writes, "Justice and peace will flow as a natural result from a genuine and appropriate concern for creation. . . . Peace is a consequence of justice. . . . Justice and peace flow naturally out of a deep respect for all of creation."[75] Indeed, peace ultimately will require the full conjunction of economic justice, human social justice, and ecojustice. Healing people (economic and social justice) and healing the earth (ecojustice) must therefore be understood as communal or relational activities, not as individualistic goals. A healing peace, or shalom, relies on the web of all interconnected life, the interplay of god/ess, people, and nature working cooperatively together. According to Carol Johnston, attaining such all-encompassing shalom, or peace-as-justice, depends "on the recognition that human persons, their communities, and the natural world are all inherently related, such that freedom and justice are dynamic dimensions of relationships characterized by participation and solidarity."[76] Shalom, peace-as-justice, cannot be achieved for the whole web of life until it is achieved throughout the whole web of life for all those whose lives constitute the oneness of life.

This recurring demand for an all-encompassing justice is also found in the prophetic and liberating minority voices that have consistently called Judaism and, later, Christianity into question from within their own ranks. James Nash assumes the appropriateness of that prophetic voice for ecological concerns when he thus insists that "there is no inherent reason why biblical concepts of justice cannot be extended to relationships between humanity and other life forms. . . . The affirmation of the rights of nature cannot be summarily dismissed."[77] In what may be characteristic of any prophetic effort coopted by heteropatriarchy, however, Nash unfortunately reduces the broader concept of justice as right-relation to the more narrow concept of rights, a reductionist concept that inevitably becomes a hierarchy of rights with humanity egocentrically on top.

On the positive side, Nash argues that the nonhuman biosphere has the right to "healthy and whole habitats" and to "freedom from human cruelty" such that "human-induced extinctions . . . should be prevented" and, to assure such prevention, such activities as recreational hunting for sport as well as commercial fur-trading and ivory-trading should be constrained, and human beings should "respect the integrity of nature by letting species and their members work out their own interactions. . . adaptations [and reproduction within] the struggle for survival, without unwarranted human protections and interventions."[78] Not only does he prophetically argue that we need to learn to live "sustainably within the bounds of the regenerative, absorptive, and carrying capacities of the earth so that all future generations can also do so indefinitely," but he also recommends that we make reparations for whenever and wherever we have failed to do so, such that we put things back in "the closest possible approximation of the original, natural interactions."[79]

On the negative side, however, these clearly positive values and recommendations notwithstanding, Nash's hierarchy is already apparent: *Humanity* can extend "its" rights to "other life forms." The "future generations" that require the earth and thus its protection are *human* generations. The earth's "regenerative, absorptive, and carrying capacities" are nothing but the necessary life-support system for a primarily valued *humanity*. As has already been examined in detail, Nash's ecological perspective is still a utilitarian, management ethic that values humanity over and above all other life and that sees all other life as a "resource," albeit as a resource to be used prudently: "Nonhuman rights can be respected in the aggregate by responsible, restrained usage. . . . Use sparingly, caringly, reverently. We can thereby minimize harm to individuals. . . . Frugality is a prime ecological virtue."[80] Frugality may be *a* prime ecological virtue for Nash, but humanity's unending access to nature as a resource is still his primary value.

In contrast to Nash's anthropocentrism, our recognition of the intrinsic value of all that is requires that our ecotheology radically ensure that the earth and all its inhabitants are treated as equal in value and thereby avoid elevating the continuation of human life to a position of greater importance or value than the continuation of life itself. The problem with speaking in terms of rights or a hierarchy of rights, as Nash does, is that the typical human-centeredness in any discourse of rights always risks "positing an inclusively arranged, but dangerously ordered, universe of competing rights" where, when "rights" conflict, nonhuman nature always loses.[81] In other words, any hierarchy of environmental or ecological rights ends up ranking the parts of nature and debating which rights apply to which nonhuman life forms; the "operative dualism" merely shifts from human/nonhuman to "sentient/nonsentient" or some other dualism that includes some life forms and excludes others.[82] Feeling and instinct are just as intrinsically valuable as intellect or sentience or any other qualifiers. To presume otherwise is once again humanly arrogant. We are reminded again that because all things are intrinsically valuable and because the divine is immanent in all life, justice as right-relation must also be extended to all things.[83] In short, a truly liberational, healing, and restorative ecological ethic must "define a whole larger than the human species."[84] As have many ecofeminists already, our gay ecotheology must reconceptualize "justice" not as a matter of so-called liberal individual human rights and freedoms with their inevitable hierarchy of competing rights by which nonhuman nature invariably loses, nor even as a matter of anthropocentric "caring," but rather as a matter of right-relatedness, of caring, cooperation, *and* responsibility, that recognizes the fundamental and utterly nonhierarchical relationality and intrinsic value of all things.[85]

Granted, the issue of justice for all life forms, our concern for caring, cooperation, *and* responsibility, and our recognition of the equal and intrinsic value of all life, does lead us into a pragmatic dilemma. To refuse to acknowledge and wrestle with that dilemma risks having our ecotheology degenerate into a futile idealism. The troublesome aspect of our human interdependence with all life and our interconnectedness in the web of being remains the reality that we do *use* portions of nature; at the very least, we are predators who require food and shelter. Recognizing this realistic dilemma, ecofeminism insists that we must come to understand "the many ways in which we can walk the fine line between using the earth as a natural resource for humans and respecting the earth's own needs, cycles, energies, and eco-systems."[86] *All* life is equally and intrinsically valuable; animals, plants, people, and the earth are *all* interrelated; *all* life is a manifestation of divine immanence such that when we do destroy a life—for food, for health care, for "pest control"—we should do so reverently, prudently, and gratefully.[87]

Disrespect and carelessness result whenever we assume that we are better than or more valuable than any life we take by causing suffering or by killing unnecessarily (e.g., hunting for sport, furring, trivial animal testing for unnecessary commodities like cosmetics). We must necessarily act in self-preserving ways, but, as has been argued throughout, that does not sanction any absolute or divinely decreed hierarchies of values or rights and it most certainly does not sanction any exploitative consumerism. It seeks, instead, to approach the compassionate wisdom of certain Native Americans who historically recognized all nonhuman nature not as objectified "others," but as subjective "thous" in the web of being who sacrifice their lives for our own: People "must necessarily hunt to live, and as long as they have a properly respectful attitude toward the animals they kill, the animals are not offended. But when [people] kill animals disrespectfully or carelessly, the animals are offended."[88]

Lois Daly has also realized the depths of our pragmatic dilemma—that we must use nature to some extent and yet that to do so when we acknowledge our intimate subjective interconnection with nature may induce guilt. As a result, she adamantly argues that "the necessity of killing or harming does not challenge the [valuational] authority of reverence for [all] life" and goes on to suggest that the varying "intensity of guilt incurred in acts that kill or harm" through human necessity (sustenance, health care, etc.) may be assuaged by the degree of necessity (food, antiviral drugs, etc.), by a grateful prudence that absolutely precludes exploitation and consumerism, and, by extension, by acts of caring, service, and justice as right-relation undertaken throughout the whole biosphere.[89] Clearly in the case of AIDS, or with other retroviral, viral, or bacterial diseases, we have to make the human life-saving choice to kill that microorganismic life that threatens human life. Some responsibly limited and compassionate animal testing for vaccines and cures may also be warranted. And, apart from such life-threatening situations, we require shelter, food, and clothing. Importantly, however, these life-preserving activities are vastly different from those activities that abuse or waste life.

At best, we can minimize the necessary harm we inflict upon the earth and its nonhuman inhabitants while also realizing, once again, that although we necessarily act in hierarchicalized or prioritized ways, such life-preserving necessity does not imply any ontologically given hierarchy of values or rights. Although as human beings we necessarily value the continuation of human life, that level of basic, necessary egocentrism should not imply that humanity is the most valuable life form in the cosmos now or ever. Or, as Daly concludes, "There is no moral hierarchy that says that decisions to destroy infectious bacteria in human beings or [to destroy] other animals [i.e., for food] are the right decisions. There is no sure way to judge any being, human or not, as less worthy and therefore insignificant enough to allow it to be killed."[90] The pragmatic dilemma that keeps the idealism of our gay ecotheology in check has no simplistic resolution. Acknowledging the fundamentally equal and intrinsic value of all that is, while also realizing that we do need and use nature, cannot be reduced to a simplistic and anthropocentric hierarchy of rights. Taking ecological responsibility squarely upon our shoulders means that we must assume the more difficult task of operating out of the abstract values of caring, cooperation, *and* responsibility and of justice as right-relation, applied and tested in every moment and in every interrelationship with all that is. These more difficult activities demand our fullest maturity in assuming the tasks of liberating and healing both peoples and the earth.

"Politics and Economics"

The complexity of liberational values and the necessary harm that human life entails again confronts us with the reality of our deep embeddedness or interconnectedness in the web of being. Nothing we do is without its reverberations throughout all of life. Everything we do has consequences. On the human level alone, liberation theologies of every sort have long realized that this also means the "personal is political." In the present context, relational and consequential complexities also lead us to realize that the personal is ecological and that the ecological is also political. Complexity begets complexity, which is richness, cosmically speaking; there will be no simple solutions. Consequently, James Nash argues that the current pluriform or complex ecological crisis requires "a high and unprecedented level of international cooperation"; moreover, "global solidarity is no longer only an ultimate vision; it is fast becoming an ecological and political necessity."[91] He further implies that we must not fragment any of our liberational pursuits, whether justice relative to gay men and lesbians, or justice relative to AIDS care, or justice relative to the earth; we must instead "pursue ecological integrity in intimate alliance with the struggles for social peace and justice"[92] for all peoples, including gay men and lesbians.

Unfortunately, just as Nash reduces justice to a hierarchy of rights, he naively believes that heteropatriarchal power-over can effectively legislate solutions. He believes that political change is more important than fundamental changes in values and life-styles—which is to say, changes in consciousness—as if legal coercion alone could successfully compel lasting change. He prefers the power-over of legal coercion to the power-with of consciousness-raising and cooperation.[93] In sharp contrast, gay liberation theology and our gay ecotheology derived from it must insist on the value of changing consciousness, of changing the ways people think and value, so that liberational and ecologically sound, reconstructed values and life-styles will not only pursue and effect political change but will also provide the basic attitudinal changes that make lasting cooperation truly possible and legislated change truly effective. Changes in both consciousness and law must go hand in hand. Ecofeminism concurs, insisting that "the methods we choose in dealing with problems must be life-affirming, consensual, and non-violent" or noncoercive.[94] Clearly, any power-over political model is rejected in favor of a power-with model, such as that which Starhawk describes:

> Time is a cycle. . . . Our model is the earth, and the seed that is planted and springs up, grows, loses life, is planted and comes up again and again and again.
>
> That. . . is the kind of model we need for our politics. We need to see the process of changing our society as a lifetime challenge and commitment. Transforming consciousness so that we can preserve and sustain the earth is a long-term project.[95]

Grounded in and inspired by our ecotheological vision, we must nurture the commitment and perseverance, the patience and fortitude, for such a worthy pursuit. We must remember to allow ourselves cycles of action and healing rest. We must avoid cynicism by appreciating what we have accomplished so far. And, we must (re)learn the grace by which god/ess shares with us these rhythms of liberational and healing change.

Inevitably in a society based on consumerism, development, and seemingly unlimited growth, that which is political is also economic. Because ecological solutions will exact economic exchanges in our political situation, politics and economics ultimately go hand in hand in both our theology and our praxis. Once again Carolyn Merchant's astute analysis can help us to understand these complex issues. With reference to the time period she has so intensively studied, she notes,

> Between 1500 and 1700 . . . a subsistence economy in which resources, goods, money, or labor were exchanged for commodities [bartering] was replaced in many areas by the open-ended accumulation of profits in an international market. Living animate nature died, while dead inanimate money was endowed with life. . . . Nature, women, blacks, and wage laborers were [endowed with] a new status as "natural" and human resources for the modern world system,[96]

while gay men and lesbians were endowed with the new status of "unnatural," as totally disposable persons.

In other words, as "production for subsistence began to be replaced by more specialized production for the market," bartering of mutually necessary goods and services was replaced by monetary exchanges, intermediaries were interposed between landed nobility and those persons actually living on the land, and the resultant stratification and alienation of the new market-oriented production led to accumulation (of money), consumerism (of commodities), and exploitation (of nature and labor), by means of which altogether "an inexorably accelerating force of expansion and accumulation [was] achieved . . . at the expense of the environment and the village community.[97] Importantly, while the earliest capitalist market economy was largely agrarian or agricultural—with people intimately tied to the land, as in the pre-Civil War rural South—increasing technology shifted production toward industrialization and society toward urbanization, displacing agrarian life. As a result, the market economy, the monetary exchange system, the accumulation of profits and property, and the mechanistic exploitation of the earth altogether undermined organic community. With simultaneous agricultural advances and rural industrialization, communal farming and communal administration of resources also dissipated.[98] Or, as Merchant herself says, "The tendency toward growth, expansion, and accumulation inherent in capitalism result[ed] in the displacement of subsistence farmers from the land and the disruption of traditional patterns of human-land interaction."[99]

The breakdown of communal living and collective subsistence economies, the displacement of persons from rural areas into urban cities, and the resulting dissolution of any "thou" relationship between people and the earth altogether fostered alienation. Organic and relational values were replaced with alienated and exploitative values; work was no longer an intimate relation with the land but had become an alienated process of production for others' profit and consumerism. Merchant is adamantly critical of this alienation of work, the artificiality of human environments, and the declining quality of life for humans and nonhumans alike that this centuries-old process has created for both capitalist and socialist countries:

> One of the most serious human problems [of] industrial capitalism [is the] alienation caused by a person's daily labor for wages. . . . Another individual reaps both money and a higher standard of living as a result. [Likewise], in modern socialist and communist societies. . . the extensive bureaucracy [management]. . . also intrudes between worker and product. The unity of a meaningful life with productive "hands-on" work [is] lost to thousands of people at the bottom of. . . society.
> . . . [Moreover], assumptions about nature push us increasingly

in the direction of artificial environments, mechanized control over more and more aspects of human life, and a loss of the quality of life itself. [100]

Neither Merchant nor Nash is willing to accept the end results of this economic process as they confront us today. From her particular perspective, Merchant argues that "a reassessment of the values and constraints historically associated with the organic worldview [is] essential for a viable future,"[101] while Nash similarly argues that, because "the ideology of economic growth... ignores the ecological reality of limits," we must immediately begin to foster "growth in human well-being rather than material productivity."[102]

Indeed, the "ideology of economic growth," which assumes that growth is an endlessly possible and desirable activity and that the natural "resources" for such endless growth are infinite, testifies all too well to the ecologically disastrous myopia of our Western mindset. Among the many problems with growth economics is the focus on "the center," the market and profits associated with individualized accumulation; peoples on the margins and damaged ecosystems are not accorded monetary value or consideration.[103] Or, as John Cobb has argued, whenever economics are viewed with anthropocentric, androcentric, or otherwise hierarchically oppressive assumptions, nonhuman nature has value only insofar as humans value it, usually in monetary terms, conditions that can only lead to exploitation (of utilitarian "resources") and expendability (of things and people deemed "useless").[104]

Heidi Hadsell extends this analysis to argue that, "given the international hierarchy of capitalism and the internal structures it creates, growth tends actually to increase rather than to decrease the inequalities of distribution both among nations and among classes within nations"; consequently, we need to address the very "logic of capitalism itself, so that first, people and second, nature are no longer treated as mere externalities of the process of accumulation."[105] One of the things we realize when we do address "the logic of capitalism" is that the conflict our government constructs between jobs (economics) and environment (ecology) is a false dichotomy employed to preclude ecojustice. George Bush, for example, virtually stripped the international Earth Summit (in Rio de Janeiro during the summer of 1992) of any proactive power to resolve environmental problems, particularly to restrict greenhouse gas emissions, based on the argument that environmental controls would eliminate jobs and almighty growth. During the subsequent 1992 election campaign, he pitted logging the Northwest's old-growth forests (jobs and economics) against the continued survival of the spotted owl whose life depends upon those forests (eco-justice), as if these two goals are mutually exclusive.

What government leaders fail to recognize is that, as Carol Johnston has argued, "instead of more crisis management and more distribution, we need inclusive participation and power sharing based on the recognition of the inherent relatedness of every entity and on [the] intrinsic value" of every entity.[106] Similarly, Cobb argues that, instead of growth and development economics, economics should be "ordered for the well-being of human communities understood to be immersed in larger natural communities whose well-being is also [intrinsically] important."[107] Again, we are brought back to ecological imagery reminiscent of that of Anne Primavesi—human systems and natural systems interact, interweave, and intertwine to form larger systems and systems of systems. All life is interconnected and interdependent; ignoring interdependence for the sake of individualized economic gain can only be ecologically destructive. Admirably, in clear opposition to our Western-style, endless growth-and-development based economic system, James Nash goes so far as to argue both that "economic conversion to ecological sustainability [is] a social, economic, and ecological necessity," and further, that "ecological protection cannot be dismissed simply as an economic liability."[108]

To place Nash's argument within the context of our gay ecotheology, ecologically prudent changes must be undertaken, even if there are no economic benefits. An ecological economics must be about the process of enhancing the intrinsic value or quality of all life, not the instrumental value or profit margin of the bio-sphere. Society and government together must cooperatively pro-vide the leadership and the means (power-with, *not* power-over) for reckoning with any consequential economic losses. "Green economists," for example, must convince our government as well as other governments "to include obvious environmental problems, such as rising carbon dioxide levels or deforestation in calculations of GNP," or gross national product; growth and development eco-nomics must be measured against environmental costs to accurately and ecologically appraise real improvements in the quality of (all) life.[109] Instead of fostering more and more growth and development (i.e., exploitation of natural "resources"), our enhanced awareness of the interdependence of all life requires that "the scale of human economics must respect the limits of [nature] and the consequences of waste," writes Carol Johnston. "Economic wisdom for the long term would assert that economics that are damaging their natural environments, thus unsustainable, are in trouble, because they cannot continue."[110]

Clearly, what the earth and its people need is not consump-tion, but healthier communities, with sufficient goods available and equally distributed so that the basic needs of everyone are met and so that present consumption becomes compatible with contin-ued, future consumption of the *necessities* for quality of life.[111] In short, says John Cobb, "Human consumption must be compatible with the continuing health of the biosphere and the relative free-dom of its individual members [both human and nonhuman] from unnecessary suffering."[112] Practically speaking, James Nash suggests that "alternatives include simpler life styles, vigorous conservation of energy and other resources, comprehensive recycling, sufficient [governmental] regulations, polluter-pays penalties, sustainable biodiversity, international cooperation, and equitable sharing of economic goods"; he goes even further out on the proverbial limb when he adds to this list "limits to growth for the affluent and eco-nomic sharing with the poor."[113]

As regards the poor, both Nash and Johnston recognize that

the Third World needs our economic assistance. After all, "it was not the needs of the poor that sacrificed environmental integrity, but economic growth for the sake of profits that rarely benefit the poor"; for example, "poor Brazilians . . . move into the rainforest *after* corporations have logged the valuable hardwoods and left a desert for the poor to try to live from."[114] Of course, enabling the Third World to achieve *American* standards of living would be an ecological disaster, while denying them access to the same "things" (i.e., same *materialistic* quality of life) we already enjoy clearly smacks of economic injustice under the guise of ecology. To skirt this dilemma, Nash suggests that we must somehow learn to balance limiting our own production and consumption with facilitating "sustainable" or ecologically friendly development for the have-nots.[115] In other words, people living in the northern hemisphere, where consumption (and accumulation of profits) is the highest, must learn to simplify our life-styles, while people living in the Third World must seek ecologically sound means to improve their own quality of life.[116] An optimal balance must be found, for the sake of justice toward the Third World and justice toward the whole earth. And, of course, the First World should already be providing the necessary leadership and ecological wisdom for these efforts rather than waiting to be prodded into doing so.

Overall, then, the complaint against heteropatriarchy and its hierarchical values that devalue and dominate (women, people of color, third-world peoples), that devalue and exploit (nature and labor), and that disvalue and exclude (Native Americans, the poor and the homeless, the mentally and physically challenged, gay men and lesbians, nonhuman nature having no apparent utilitarian value, and diversity in general) invariably comes down to a critique of economics and the current failure of individualistic economics—growth and development, accumulation, and consumerism. While economic analyses per se may be outside the traditional theologian's expected expertise, our gay ecotheology can at the very least demand economic wisdom, prudence and charity, and justice as right-relation, personally, corporately, and politically, for all people, including gay men and lesbians, and for all the earth and all its nonhuman inhabitants as well. Merchant astutely synthesizes her own ecofeminism and Nash's economic reflections in her similar overall response:

> *Both the women's movement and the ecology movement are sharply critical of the costs of competition, aggression, and domination arising from the market economy's modus operandi in nature and society. Ecology has been . . . subversive . . . in its criticism of the consequences of uncontrolled growth associated with capitalism, technology, and progress.* [117]

The vast complexities of the processes of patriarchy, Christianization, and mechanization that have brought us and our earth—our home—to our present state of crisis require equally complex analyses and reconstructions. While such complexity may at first overwhelm us, the urgency of the earth's cry for our subjective, relational response will not allow us to pursue too easy or simplistic solutions doomed to failure. Indeed, Merchant, Nash, and others have already suggested alternative ways of thinking and acting, however abstract or specific they may be, to start us in the right direction. As we begin to appreciate the interconnections of the theological, the sociopolitical, and the economic, we need not be overwhelmed insofar as we can also realize the quiet, empowering centering that is god/ess-with-us and that, as such, will enable us to pursue our own subversive and ecologically wise activity or praxis, informed by our gay ecotheology and nurtured by our intimate relationship with divinely immanent life itself, throughout all the earth.

Ruby Slippers, Home, and Our Own Backyard

Within each of us there is an Owl, a Rabbit, an Eeyore, and a Pooh. For too long, we have chosen the way of Owl and Rabbit. Now, like Eeyore, we complain about the results. But that accomplishes nothing. If we are smart, we will choose the way of Pooh. As if from far away, it calls to us with the voice of a child's mind. It may be hard to hear at times, but it is important just the same, because without it, we will never find our way through the Forest.

—Benjamin Hoff, *The Tao of Pooh*

Given the vast complexity of the processes of heteropatriarchy, imperialist Christianity, and mechanization, as well as the complexity of the human injustice and ecological devastation that have resulted from their collusion, we may indeed find ourselves feeling overwhelmed, wishing as it were that we could click together the heels of our ruby slippers and return to some pristine land of pure justice as right-relation among all things. Women would not be sexistly categorized as either good witches or bad witches. Gay men and lesbians would not be homophobically excluded from any of life's possibilities. The land would not be patriarchically dominated and exploited nor the animals treated as disposable commodities. No plant or animal species would ever become extinct because of human actions, and AIDS simply would not exist. As we realize, however, that such wishful thinking is just another form of transcendent escapism, we are brought back abruptly to the reality of our ghettos and our far less than pristine emerald cities: no benevolent wizard, no helium-filled balloon, no ruby slippers, just reality, here and now.

We cannot escape the homophobia that disvalues gay and lesbian lives and that, projected onto the environment and sustained by insensitive governmental policies, devalues all the earth and disvalues all diversity and all nonhuman and nonutilitarian life. And, quite naturally, we are angered and frustrated by these hard realities. As a result, we can either get stuck in our despairing, paralyzing anger and do nothing, or find in our righteous anger the empowering energy of god/ess-with-us. Even so, we must still allow ourselves cycles of rest and healing, as well as of action and polemic. We must remember with Starhawk that time is our model;[1] the quest for liberation and healing is not some linear, goal-directed journey toward an end-time, but it is rather a process interwoven with the cycles of our lives, here and now. The wisdom of Ecclesiastes reminds us that there are times for polemic and for actions writ large and there are also times for inner contemplation, for rest, and for actions undertaken in the smaller space of our lives and our homes. In his introduction to the new edition of Henry David Thoreau's *Walking*, John Elder elegantly elaborates:

> *The disasters of our global environmental crisis will certainly*
> *make rage and polemic increasingly central parts of our nature writing.*
> *But by the same token we will need to continue finding consolation in*
> *the sunset, and to discover within settled landscapes and cities*
> *visions of nature's wholeness that can inspire a personal and social*
> *conversion. . . starting, perhaps, with the hopefulness in which we set*
> *out on our walks.*[2]

We are in a very real sense brought back to our own neighborhoods and parks where we walk, to our own backyards where we relax and putter, and to our own homes where we live. In revaluing our homes, Cynthia Hamilton has shown the extent to which, particularly in minority communities, environmental action to ensure the safety of the home and its immediate neighborhood environment often precedes a deeper ecological awareness.[3] Local crises facilitate consciousness-raising, which in turn enables us to make the connections between our neighborhoods and the larger global community. As we do experience our consciousness changing—as we realize the absolutely equal and intrinsic value of all that is, as well as the fundamental interconnectedness, relationality, and interdependence of all things within the web of being—we cannot help but question the human arrogance that has permeated our society and culture until now. We are in fact compelled to exchange egocentrism for ecocentrism, to exchange anthropocentrism for what Anne Primavesi has termed "ecological humility."[4]

Within the context of a gay ecotheology that critically surveys Judaism and Christianity as a two-pronged tradition without endorsing any particular institutional form of that tradition, "ecological humility" can nonetheless be understood as part and parcel of an important Jewish concept. The concept of *tikkun olam* entails our obligation to be about the business of repairing the world, in its human and nonhuman, its biospheric and geospheric aspects. It does not assume that humanity is the pinnacle of creation, but rather celebrates the intrinsic value and rich diversity of all that is and reminds us of our humble interdependence within the web of being. *Tikkun olam* therefore also requires that we assume the tasks of caring, cooperation, *and* responsibility and of justice as right-relation throughout the earth. It is our obligation to love the earth and to love life itself, even though we are mortal and our individual lives must end.[5]

Both "ecological humility" and *tikkun olam* also remind us that, although we have no right to elevate our humanity over the rest of creation, our human lives do make a difference. Our actions in the larger sociopolitical arena and our actions at home are equally valuable. If we overlook the ecological impact of our individual lives, we also overlook a profound source of empowerment and we fail to connect our lives with life itself, that is, with the global dimensions of ecological concerns. Julia Scofield Russell insightfully says:

Another level of empowerment, commitment, and opportunity...
is often overlooked when we discuss social change... the essential
role our individual life styles, our everyday choices and behavior,
play in maintaining the status quo or effecting change.... Lasting
societal transformation begins with and rests on transformation of the
individual.[6]

An ecologically sound theology-as-praxis confronts us and begins with us "in our own backyards," that is, in our own lives and homes and communities.

In some respects as a larger community, gay men and lesbians may be behind other groups in wrestling with ecological issues and environmental causes because our energies are so consumed, and necessarily so, in dealing with AIDS and in dealing with homophobia, both as antigay/lesbian violence and as other forms of oppression, such as professional barriers, outright job discrimination, no legal protections or benefits for couples—and the list could go on. Even with our considerable in-house agenda, which absolutely must not be forsaken, groups such as Gays United Against Nuclear Arms have pursued ecological concerns, while individuals have worked within local neighborhood groups on similar issues. In Atlanta, for example, gay men and lesbians have been active in fighting unnecessary freeways and trucking facilities that threaten our neighborhoods and their immediate ecosystems. Leaving our psychological or epistemological ghettos does not mean relinquishing our very important gay liberation agenda; it does mean developing a broader vision that sees the connections among all forms of oppression, exploitation, and disvaluation and that thereby facilitates liaisons to confront all of these. Not through cooptation, but through cooperation, working together to achieve liberation for all peoples and the earth itself, will we achieve our own liberation.

Apart from community efforts, our individual lives also make a difference. My spouse and I, for example, have had to realize that at some level, we are basically lazy; we are not likely to undertake a life-style change that becomes a major ordeal, unless the underlying values are truly compelling and the potential results are really worth the effort. Consequently, although our home is far from 100-percent ecologically sound, at the same time we feel that anything we are doing could not be too difficult for anyone else to do as well. In a sense, the simple things we are already doing may serve as easy examples for others. At work, we recycle paper products, including our phone books, use recycled paper goods, and encourage others to do the same—even though, currently, recycled goods cost our offices more than "dead-tree" paper. Making double-sided photocopies saves paper. I even started getting my lunch cola in a paper hot drink cup (no styrofoam!) so I can use the same cup for the coffee I take back to work. If you multiply five days a week by fifty weeks, that one behavioral change will save 250 paper cups (and comparable tree parts) a year! We own a fuel efficient car (I traded in a used car in part because I was embarrassed by its mileage and in part because I was troubled by its oppressive, consumerist image), we plan trips that avoid backtracking and wasting gas, and we try to avoid sudden bursts of gasoline consumption.

Again, however, we've found that what we do at home is the most substantive. Our house itself is not new construction, with all the baggage of growth economics that entails, but is some fifty years old, recycled through all its previous owners down to us. The majority of our furniture is also "recycled," inexpensive depression era pieces termed "antiques" by the trendy; no trees were newly sacrificed just for us here, either. We recycle plastics, newspapers, glass, phone books, and even the Christmas tree—planting dogwood trees in its honor—and plan trips to the currently scattered locations for our different recyclables in order to save gas. We use low-watt bulbs and a water-saving shower head. We keep the water heater turned low (but comfortable—and turned off during our trips away from home), we turn off unnecessary lights, we run both air conditioning and heat at prudent temperatures, and we leave both turned off when we're not home during the day. We use phosphate-free detergent and try to keep the house free of chemicals, using the plunger instead of a chemical drain opener, for example. We try to avoid consumerism and to be wise consumers—by looking for recycled packaging and environmentally safe products from coffee filters to toilet paper, by reading labels and avoiding chemicals, and by avoiding certain foods and double-checking others (veal has become morally repugnant and tuna must be dolphin safe). We support environmentally friendly advocacy organizations with very modest subscriptions, purchasing their catalogue items for holiday gifts rather than department store commodities. We write letters, make phone calls, and support local groups that wrestle with some ecological issue. And we *vote*—we vote ecologically minded as well as determined to pursue gay- and AIDS-related issues.

Outdoors we refuse to send our leaves to a landfill and have started our own composting instead. We use peat moss in the garden and we use minimal fertilizers and insecticides—purchasing only those that are environmentally friendly and using them in a very limited way. Instead of spraying insecticides around the yard, we have used cedar chips for our dogs' bedding area and we recycle those chips as mulch for plants when they loose their effectiveness against the fleas. We raise many of our own vegetables and we've healed and nurtured nearly exhausted old plants and added new plants to our yard. When we water the plants and garden, we make sure that rain is not already imminent and then do so at night to avoid evaporation.

Importantly, none of these examples is offered as any sort of pat on *our* backs; that would just be hubris again. Rather, as we have talked about these things, we have come to feel that if they were not too difficult for us, then they might be good starting places for others as well. We know that we ourselves must always learn to do more; we need to become even wiser consumers, ecologically speaking, and to keep our latent consumerist tendencies under control (our tight budget helps!). But we are trying and all our best efforts do make a difference. For us, undertaking these activities helps us not to feel overwhelmed; they encourage us to keep learning, to keep voting appropriately, and to keep acting ever more appropriately. Neither gay liberation theology nor gay eco-theology is just an intellectual exercise; it is instead a way of being and living in the world and with the world. Theology *is* praxis, so these become partial fulfillments of our obligation to love the earth.

Although as HIV-positive individuals we are very aware of our mortality, we nevertheless love life itself, even though we know our individual lives will end at some point. Our own imminent ends, whenever they may come, are no reason to exploit or other-wise disvalue any other life. The urgency of our lives in the midst of homophobia and AIDS, and the urgency of the earth's ecological crises as well, has not led us to wall ourselves off in a ghetto or to seek escapist solutions. Instead, they have opened the ghetto's gates and revealed a broader, richer, ecological perspective that ab-solutely affirms life—being itself—as good. This is our *tikkun olam*. This is god/ess-with-us. Moreover, with these affirmations, we share a credo and a call to action already elegantly articulated by Carol Christ:

> *We come from the earth and to the earth we shall return. Life feeds on life. We live because others die, and we will die so that others may live. The divinity that shapes our ends is life, death, and change, understood both literally and as a metaphor for our daily lives. . . . Knowledge that we are but a small part of life and death and transformation is the essential religious insight. The essential religious response is to rejoice and to weep, to sing and to dance. . . in praise of an existence far more complicated, more intricate, more enduring that we are.*
>
> *. . . It is life that can end in death at any moment that we must love.* [7]

Life calls us to life, to liberation, and to healing the earth.

Notes

▼

PREFACE

1. J. Michael Clark, "Prophecy, Subjectivity, and Theodicy in Gay Theology: Developing a Constructive Methodology" (on feminist paradigms), and Thomas M. Thurston, "Gay Theology of Liberation and the Hermeneutic Circle" (on Latin American liberation theology paradigms), in *Constructing Gay Theology*, Gay Men's Issues in Religious Studies Series, ed. M. L. Stemmeler and J. M. Clark, vol. 2 (Dallas: Monument Press, 1991), 27–44 and 7–26, respectively.

2. E. Michael Gorman, "A Special Window: An Anthropological Perspective on Spirituality in Contemporary U.S. Gay Male Culture," in *Constructing Gay Theology*, 45–61; Ronald E. Long and J. Michael Clark, *AIDS, God, and Faith: Continuing the Dialogue on Constructing Gay Theology* (Dallas: Monument Press, 1992).

3. The full progression of the author's work to date includes the following, listed chronologically by category: socioliterary criticism—*Liberation and Disillusionment: The Development of Gay Male Criticism and Popular Fiction a Decade after Stonewall* (Las Colinas, TX: The Liberal Press, 1987), *Pink Triangles and Gay Images: (Re)claiming Communal and Personal History in Retrospective Gay Fiction* (Arlington, TX: Liberal Arts Press, 1987); spiritual autobiography—*Diary of a Southern Queen: An HIV+ Vision Quest* (Dallas: Monument Press, 1990), *Southern Gothic: Of Remembering and Releasing* (Irving, TX: Scholars Books, 1991); theology and ethics—*Gay Being, Divine Presence: Essays in Gay Spirituality* (Garland, TX: Tangelwüld Press, 1987), *A Place to Start: Toward an Unapologetic Gay Liberation Theology* (Dallas: Monu-

ment Press, 1989), *A Defiant Celebration: Theological Ethics and Gay Sexuality* (Garland, TX: Tangelwüld Press, 1990), *A Lavender Cosmic Pilgrim: Further Ruminations on Gay Spirituality, Theology, and Sexuality* (Las Colinas, TX: The Liberal Press, 1990), *Theologizing Gay: Fragments of Liberation Activity* (Oak Cliff, TX: Minuteman Press, 1991), *Masculine Socialization and Gay Liberation: A Conversation on the Work of James Nelson and Other Wise Friends* (with Bob McNeir; Las Colinas, TX: The Liberal Press, 1992), *AIDS, God, and Faith* (see note 2).

4. Clark and McNeir, *Masculine Socialization;* cf. Al Cotton, "Foreword: On Gay Curmudgeons and Buccaneers," in Clark, *Diary,* v-viii.

5. Clark, *Diary,* 78.

CHAPTER 1

1. Clark, *Liberation and Disillusionment,* 1, and *A Place to Start,* 1.

2. Clark, *Liberation and Disillusionment,* 2.

3. Anne Primavesi, *From Apocalypse to Genesis: Ecology, Feminism and Christianity* (Minneapolis: Fortress Press, 1991), 110.

4. Ibid., 130.

5. Judith Plaskow and Carol P. Christ, "Introduction," in *Weaving the Visions: New Patterns in Feminist Spirituality,* ed. J. Plaskow and C. P. Christ (San Francisco: Harper and Row, 1989), 6; cf. Clark, *A Lavender Cosmic Pilgrim,* 3.

6. Clark and McNeir, *Masculine Socialization,* 13–20.

7. Judith Plant, "Searching for Common Ground: Ecofeminism and Bioregionalism," in *Reweaving the World: The Emergence of Eco-feminism,* ed. I. Diamond and G. F. Orenstein (San Francisco: Sierra Club Books, 1990), 160, 161.

8. Ibid., 160.

9. Primavesi, *From Apocalypse to Genesis,* 24.

10. Ibid., 52.

11. Ibid., 152.

12. Julia Scofield Russell, "The Evolution of an Ecofeminist," in *Reweaving the World,* 228.

13. Ibid.

14. In a single issue of *International Wildlife* (21, no. 6 [November-December 1991]), the "Wildlife Digest" listed the following concerns (25,

28): "poachers who kill rare [Pacific yew trees] up to 200 years old by indiscriminately stripping their bark," which yields a cancer-fighting drug; "more than 80% of Americans believe environmental damage is the most serious crime businesses commit"; one oil company "announced recently that it has produced a cleaner-burning gasoline that reduces some pollutants by more than a third but does not plan to market it until required to . . . in 1996"; "overfishing and pollution have so decimated the nation's marine fisheries that one-third of all fish species declined in the past decade. . . . At least 14 species are in serious decline"; "Florida panthers . . . are now functionally extinct in the Everglades. . . . Only an estimated 30–50 Florida panthers remain in the wild throughout the state"; "Unless poaching and habitat loss are checked soon, the giant panda has little chance of surviving much longer in the wild. . . . Panda pelts are so prized in Taiwan and Japan that even China's death penalty for poachers has done little to deter panda poachers, who can earn several years' income by trading a few pelts." The issue also included a very disturbing article on the continuing use of humanly and environmentally hazardous agricultural chemicals in the third world: Bruce Selcraig, "Costa Rica's Lethal Harvest," 21–24.

15. Cf. Clark, *A Place to Start*.

16. Primavesi, *From Apocalypse to Genesis*, 156.

17. Ibid., 64.

18. James A. Nash, *Loving Nature: Ecological Integrity and Christian Responsibility* (Nashville: Abingdon Press, 1991), 149, 150, 151, 166, 173, respectively.

19. Cf. Carolyn Merchant, *The Death of Nature: Women, Ecology, and the Scientific Revolution* (1980; San Francisco: Harper and Row, 1989), 144, 294.

20. Primavesi, *From Apocalypse to Genesis*, 43.

21. Merchant, *The Death of Nature*, 132–43.

22. Ibid., 128.

23. Ibid., 138.

24. Ibid.

25. Cf. Primavesi, *From Apocalypse to Genesis*, 36–43; Kath Weston, *Families We Choose: Lesbians, Gays, Kinship* (New York: Columbia University Press, 1991), 27, 33–41, 165–93.

26. Michael Zimmerman, "Deep Ecology and Ecofeminism: The Emerging Dialogue," in *Reweaving the World*, 152.

27. Marti Kheel, "Ecofeminism and Deep Ecology: Reflections on Identity and Difference," in *Reweaving the World*, 129.

28. Primavesi, *From Apocalypse to Genesis*, 37.

29. Clark, *A Place to Start*, 65–78; Ronald E. Long, "God through Gay Men's Eyes: Gay Theology in the Age of AIDS," in *AIDS, God, and Faith*, 1–21.

30. See the assembled reports by W. F. Keegan, D. D. Davis, H. J. Viola, et al., in commemoration of the Columbus quintcentenary in *Archaeology* 45, no. 1 (January-February 1992): 45–59.

31. Rosemary Radford Ruether, *Liberation Theology* (New York: Paulist Press, 1972), 13, 16, 32, 34; cf. Clark, *Gay Being, Divine Presence*, 26.

32. Clark and McNeir, *Masculine Socialization*.

33. Kheel, "Ecofeminism and Deep Ecology," 131.

CHAPTER 2

1. Clark, *A Place to Start*, 11–45.

2. Brian Swimme, "How to Heal a Lobotomy," in *Reweaving the World*, 15–16.

3. Russell, "The Evolution of an Ecofeminist," 225.

4. Nancy R. Howell, "Living with the Matrix: An Ecofeminist Alternative to Hierarchy" (Paper presented at the Religion and Ecology Consultation, American Academy of Religion, Kansas City, 23 November 1991), 4.

5. Ibid., 5.

6. Ibid., 6.

7. Irene Diamond and Gloria Feman Orenstein, "Introduction," in *Reweaving the World*, ix-x.

8. Primavesi, *From Apocalypse to Genesis*, 42.

9. Ibid., 62.

10. Ibid., 101.

11. Ynestra King, "Healing the Wounds: Feminism, Ecology, and the Nature/Culture Dualism," in *Reweaving the World*, 108.

12. Judith Plant, "Toward a New World: An Introduction," in *Healing the Wounds: The Promise of Ecofeminism*, ed. J. Plant (Philadelphia: New Society Publishers, 1989), 2.

13. Primavesi, *From Apocalypse to Genesis*, 16.

14. Nash, *Loving Nature*, 106.

15. Clark, *A Place to Start*, 45–52; Long, "God through Gay Men's Eyes," 1–21.

16. Henry David Thoreau, "Walking," *Nature/Walking*, ed. J. Elder (1862. Boston: Beacon Press, 1991), 104.

17. Ibid., 115.

18. Ibid., 110.

19. Ibid., 80.

20. Cf. Primavesi, *From Apocalypse to Genesis*, 30–33; Nash, *Loving Nature*, 68.

21. Primavesi, *From Apocalypse to Genesis*, 23.

22. Nash, *Loving Nature*, 74.

23. Thomas Berry, "The Spirituality of the Earth," in *Liberating Life: Contemporary Approaches to Ecological Theology*, ed. C. Birch, W. Eakin, and J. B. McDaniel (Maryknoll, NY: Orbis Books, 1990), 151.

24. George E. Tinker, "Creation as Kin: An American Indian View," in *After Nature's Revolt: Eco-Justice and Theology*, ed. D. T. Hessel (Minneapolis: Fortress Press, 1992), 153.

25. Primavesi, *From Apocalypse to Genesis*, 79.

26. Ibid., 80, 88.

27. Ibid., 102, 103, 106.

28. Ibid., 215, 219.

29. Nash, *Loving Nature*, 74.

30. Ibid., 88, 89.

31. Ibid., 90.

32. William H. MacLeish, "From Sea to Shining Sea: 1492," *Smithsonian* 22, no. 8 (November 1991): 34–49; cf. Charles Hudson, *The Southeastern Indians* (1976. Knoxville: University of Tennessee Press, 1989), 82.

33. Hudson, *The Southeastern Indians*, 41.

34. Ibid., 19.

35. Cf. Sylvia A. Earle, "Persian Gulf Pollution: Assessing the Damage One Year Later," *National Geographic* 181, no. 2 (February 1992): 122–34.

36. Nash, *Loving Nature*, 120.

37. Ibid., 75.

38. Charlene Spretnak, "Ecofeminism: Our Roots and Flowering," in *Reweaving the World*, 11.

39. Merchant, *The Death of Nature*.

40. Ibid., 2, 28, 43; cf. 7, 23, 41.

41. Ibid., 5, 16.

42. Ibid., 67, 43, 61, 63.

43. Ibid., 68, 97.

44. Ibid., 69.

45. Ibid., 103, 238, 252, 245, 246.

46. Ibid., 252, 235.

47. Ibid., 127–28.

48. Ibid., 172, 189, 171; cf. Howell, "Living with the Matrix," 6.

49. Merchant, *The Death of Nature*, 192; cf. 234.

50. Rosemary Radford Ruether, "Toward an Ecological-Feminist Theology of Nature," in *Healing the Wounds*, 146.

51. Berry, "The Spirituality of the Earth," 154, emphasis added.

52. Cf. Merchant, *The Death of Nature*, 193, 214, 216, 228.

53. Ibid., 193, 227.

54. Ibid., xxii, 2, xxi.

55. Primavesi, *From Apocalypse to Genesis*, 196.

56. Ibid., 61.

57. Riane Eisler, "The Gaia Tradition and the Partnership Future: An Ecofeminist Manifesto," in *Reweaving the World*, 28.

58. Ibid., 33.

59. H. Paul Santmire, "Healing the Protestant Mind: Beyond the Theology of Human Dominion," in *After Nature's Revolt*, 75.

60. Martha Ellen Stortz, "Ethics, Conservation, and Theology in Ecological Perspective," *Covenant for a New Creation: Ethics, Religion, and Public Policy*, ed. C. S. Robb and C. J. Casebolt (Maryknoll, NY: Orbis Books, 1991), 204–5.

61. Nash, *Loving Nature*, 106.

62. Spretnak, "Ecofeminism," 9.

63. Santmire, "Healing the Protestant Mind," 73.

64. Primavesi, *From Apocalypse to Genesis*, 63–64.

65. Stortz, "Ethics, Conservation, and Theology," 205.

66. Primavesi, *From Apocalypse to Genesis*, 107; cf. 16.

67. Ibid., 228, 219.

68. Ibid., 205.

69. Ibid., 231–32, 243.

70. Nash, *Loving Nature*, 101; cf. George H. Kehm, "The New Story: Redemption as Fulfillment of Creation," in *After Nature's Revolt*, 93, and Di-

eter T. Hessel, "Introduction: Eco-Justice Theology after Nature's Revolt," in *After Nature's Revolt*, 2, 11.

71. Philip Hefner, "Nature's History as our History: A Proposal for Spirituality," in *After Nature's Revolt*, 183.

72. Clark, *A Place to Start*, 79–97, 105.

73. Catherine Keller, "Women against Wasting the World: Notes on Eschatology and Ecology," in *Reweaving the World*, 257.

74. Ibid., 260; cf. 257.

75. Ibid., 250, 255.

76. Primavesi, *From Apocalypse to Genesis*, 76.

77. Ruether, "Toward an Ecological-Feminist Theology of Nature," 149.

78. Carol Johnston, "Economics, Eco-Justice, and the Doctrine of God," in *After Nature's Revolt*, 154.

79. Yaakov Jerome Garb, "Perspective or Escape? Ecofeminist Musings on Contemporary Earth Imagery," in *Reweaving the World*, 272.

80. Ibid., 273.

81. Ibid.; cf. 274.

CHAPTER 3

1. Cf. Primavesi, *From Apocalypse to Genesis*, 86.

2. Swimme, "How to Heal a Lobotomy," 20.

3. Clark, *A Place to Start*, 55–65; cf. Clark, *Theologizing Gay*, 35–59.

4. Clark, *A Place to Start*, 65–78, and J. Michael Clark, "AIDS, Death, and God: Gay Liberational Theology and the Problem of Suffering," *Journal of Pastoral Counseling* 21, no. 1 (1986): 40–54.

5. Sallie McFague, "Imaging a Theology of Nature: The World as God's Body," in *Liberating Life*, 213.

6. Ibid., 209, 211.

7. Ibid., 204; cf. Sallie McFague, *Models of God: Theology for an Ecological, Nuclear Age* (Philadelphia: Fortress Press, 1987).

8. Howell, "Living with the Matrix," 21.

9. Hessel, "Introduction," 15.

10. Long, "God through Gay Men's Eyes," 14.

11. J. Michael Clark, "Toward a Lavender Credo: From Theology to Belief," in *AIDS, God, and Faith*, 57–60.

12. Cf. Garb, "Perspective or Escape?" 264–78.

13. Spretnak, "Ecofeminism," 5.

14. Ibid., 7.

15. Ruether, "Toward an Ecological-Feminist Theology of Nature," 146–47.

16. Ibid., 147, 148.

17. Primavesi, *From Apocalypse to Genesis,* 12.

18. Nash, *Loving Nature,* 65.

19. Carol P. Christ, "Rethinking Theology and Nature," in *Reweaving the World,* 58.

20. Hudson, *The Southeastern Indians,* 159.

21. Tinker, "Creation as Kin," 145; cf. 153.

22. Starhawk, "Power, Authority, and Mystery: Ecofeminism and Earth-based Spirituality," in *Reweaving the World,* 73, 74.

23. Christ, "Rethinking Theology and Nature," 69, 68, 67.

24. Diamond and Orenstein, "Introduction," xi.

25. Irene Diamond, "Babies, Heroic Experts, and a Poisoned Earth," in *Reweaving the World,* 209.

26. Keller, "Women against Wasting the World," 257.

27. Primavesi, *From Apocalypse to Genesis,* 22.

28. Ibid., 19.

29. Berry, "The Spirituality of the Earth," 151.

30. Ibid., 154, 158, 155.

31. Primavesi, *From Apocalypse to Genesis,* 54; for a more detailed elucidation of the relationship of sexuality and justice in feminist and gay liberation theologies, see J. Michael Clark, "Men's Studies, Feminist Theology, and Gay Male Sexuality," *The Journal of Men's Studies* 1, no. 2 (November 1992): 127, 145–47; cf. Carter Heyward, *Touching our Strength: The Erotic as Power and the Love of God* (San Francisco: Harper and Row, 1989).

32. Primavesi, *From Apocalypse to Genesis,* 220, 221.

33. Christ, "Rethinking Theology and Nature," 66.

34. Ibid., 67.

35. Lois K. Daly, "Ecofeminism, Reverence for Life, and Feminist Theological Ethics," in *Liberating Life,* 91.

36. Primavesi, *From Apocalypse to Genesis,* 49; Daly, "Ecofeminism," 93; Marti Kheel, "Ecofeminism and Deep Ecology," 137.

37. Howell, "Living with the Matrix," 20, 18.

38. Primavesi, *From Apocalypse to Genesis,* 245.

39. Kheel, "Ecofeminism and Deep Ecology," 136–37.

40. Ibid., 136; cf. Nash, *Loving Nature,* 180.

41. Hessel, "Introduction," 7, emphasis added.

42. Keller, "Women against Wasting the World," 259, 261.

43. Daly, "Ecofeminism," 105.

44. Merchant, *The Death of Nature,* 96.

45. Howell, "Living with the Matrix," 25; cf. 26.

46. Tinker, "Creation as Kin," 147–48.

47. Ibid., 148.

48. Primavesi, *From Apocalypse to Genesis,* 54, 155, emphasis added.

49. Howell, "Living with the Matrix," 14, 15, emphasis added.

50. Ibid., 16, 21.

51. Nash, *Loving Nature,* 66.

52. Stortz, "Ethics, Conservation, and Theology," 196.

53. Nash, *Loving Nature,* 100.

54. Ibid., 182.

55. Stortz, "Ethics, Conservation, and Theology," 197, 198.

56. McFague, "Imaging a Theology of Nature," 217, emphasis added.

57. Cynthia Hamilton, "Women, Home, and Community: The Struggle in an Urban Environment," in *Reweaving the World,* 215.

58. Ibid.

59. Susan Griffin, "Curves along the Road," in *Reweaving the World,* 95.

60. Vandana Shiva, "Development as a New Project of Western Patriarchy," in *Reweaving the World,* 193.

61. Ibid., 195.

62. Ibid., 192, 199.

63. Pamela Philipose, "Women Act: Women and Environmental Protection in India," in *Healing the Wounds,* 68–70; Primavesi, *From Apocalypse to Genesis,* 21, 58–59.

64. Clark, *A Place to Start,* 34–35, 46, 90.

65. Nash, *Loving Nature,* 117.

66. McFague, "Imaging a Theology of Nature," 217.

67. Cf. Tinker, "Creation as Kin," 148.

68. Nash, *Loving Nature,* 119.

69. Primavesi, *From Apocalypse to Genesis,* 235.

70. Cf. Nash, *Loving Nature,* 122–24.

71. Carol S. Robb, "The Rights of Farmers, the Common Good, and Feminist Questions," in *Covenant for a New Creation*, 288.

72. Starhawk, "Power, Authority, and Mystery," 82, 83; cf. Nash, *Loving Nature*, 172.

73. Ruether, "Toward an Ecological-Feminist Theology of Nature," 149.

74. Hessel, "Introduction," 9.

75. Tinker, "Creation as Kin," 146

76. Johnston, "Economics," 158; cf. 155ff.

77. Nash, *Loving Nature*, 163, 175.

78. Ibid., 187, 188.

79. Ibid., 210, 188.

80. Ibid., 183.

81. Stortz, "Ethics, Conservation, and Theology," 201.

82. Daly, "Ecofeminism," 93.

83. Cf. ibid., 94, 96.

84. Stortz, "Ethics, Conservation, and Theology," 201.

85. Cf. Santmire, "Healing the Protestant Mind," 75–77.

86. Diamond and Orenstein, "Introduction," xii.

87. Cf. Daly, "Ecofeminism," 99.

88. Hudson, *The Southeastern Indians*, 156.

89. Daly, "Ecofeminism," 101.

90. Ibid., 99.

91. Nash, *Loving Nature*, 216, 217.

92. Ibid., 217.

93. Cf. ibid., 194–95.

94. Diamond and Orenstein, "Introduction," xii.

95. Starhawk, "Power, Authority, and Mystery," 78.

96. Merchant, *The Death of Nature*, 288.

97. Ibid., 51.

98. Ibid., 78; cf. 57.

99. Ibid., 52.

100. Ibid., 87, 291; cf. 57.

101. Ibid., 289.

102. Nash, *Loving Nature*, 200, 201.

103. Johnston, "Economics," 160.

104. John B. Cobb, Jr., "Postmodern Christianity in Quest of Eco-

Justice," in *After Nature's Revolt*, 36; it should be noted that, like Anne Primavesi, Cobb unabashedly espouses Christian exclusivity (see 26) and, not unlike James Nash, he creates a scale or hierarchy with grades of "intrinsic" values that sound more like "instrumental" values, relative to whatever is higher or lower (more or less expendable) on that scale (see 33–35); nonetheless, certain of his insights are valuable for our gay ecotheology, just as are most of those of Primavesi and even many of those of Nash.

105. Heidi Hadsell, "Eco-Justice and Liberation Theology: The Priority of Human Well-Being," in *After Nature's Revolt*, 84, 85; as her title suggests, Latin American liberation theology is not without its problems for gay ecotheology as herein conceived, insofar as it does retain a very clear anthropocentrism or human priority that values nonhuman nature instrumentally rather than intrinsically: "Nature in and of itself, unrelated to human life is not valued. . . . [Nature] is viewed primarily as having instrumental value rather than intrinsic value" (82); nevertheless, Hadsell's critique of capitalist consumerism is still valid.

106. Johnston, "Economics," 161.

107. Cobb, "Postmodern Christianity," 37.

108. Nash, *Loving Nature*, 200–201, 198.

109. John Carey, "Will Saving People Save Our Planet?" *International Wildlife* 22, no. 3 (May-June 1992), 23, 16.

110. Johnston, "Economics," 165, cf. 170.

111. Cobb, "Postmodern Christianity," 37.

112. Ibid.

113. Nash, *Loving Nature*, 201, 203.

114. Johnston, "Economics," 163.

115. Nash, *Loving Nature*, 203.

116. Carey, "Will Saving People Save Our Planet?" 20.

117. Merchant, *The Death of Nature*, xx, emphasis added.

CHAPTER 4

1. Starhawk, "Power, Authority, and Mystery," 78.

2. John Elder, "Introduction: Sauntering toward the Holy Land," in *Nature/Walking*, xviii.

3. Hamilton, "Women, Home, and Community," 216.

4. Primavesi, *From Apocalypse to Genesis*, 22.

5. Roger S. Gottlieb, "Weapons of the Spirit: Jewish Resources in the Struggle against the Environmental Crisis," roundtable presentation, American Academy of Religion, Kansas City, 25 November 1991, 7–8.

6. Russell, "The Evolution of an Ecofeminist," 226.

7. Christ, "Rethinking Theology and Nature," 65–66, 67.

Selected Bibliography
▼

Birch, Charles, William Eakin, and Jay B. McDaniel, eds. *Liberating Life: Contemporary Approaches to Ecological Theology.* Maryknoll, NY: Orbis Books, 1990.

Clark, J. Michael. *A Place to Start: Toward an Unapologetic Gay Liberation Theology.* Dallas: Monument Press, 1989.

Diamond, Irene, and Gloria Feman Orenstein, eds. *Reweaving the World: The Emergence of Ecofeminism.* San Francisco: Sierra Club Books, 1990.

Emerson, Ralph Waldo, and Henry David Thoreau. *Nature/Walking,* edited by J. Elder. 1862. Boston: Beacon Press, 1991.

Hessel, Dieter T., ed. *After Nature's Revolt: Eco-Justice and Theology.* Minneapolis: Fortress Press, 1992.

Hoff, Benjamin. *The Tao of Pooh.* New York: E. P. Dutton, 1982.

Hudson, Charles. *The Southeastern Indians.* 1976. Knoxville: University of Tennessee Press, 1989.

Merchant, Carolyn. *The Death of Nature: Women, Ecology, and the Scientific Revolution.* 1980. San Francisco: Harper and Row, 1989.

Nash, James A. *Loving Nature: Ecological Integrity and Christian Responsibility.* Nashville: Abingdon Press, 1991.

Plant, Judith, ed. *Healing the Wounds: The Promise of Ecofeminism.* Philadelphia: New Society Publishers, 1989.

Primavesi, Anne. *From Apocalypse to Genesis: Ecology, Feminism and Christianity.* Minneapolis: Fortress Press, 1991.

Robb, Carol S., and Carl J. Casebolt, eds. *Covenant for a New Creation: Ethics, Religion, and Public Policy.* Maryknoll, NY: Orbis Books, 1991.

Ruether, Rosemary Radford. *Gaia and God: An Ecofeminist Theology of Earth Healing.* San Francisco: HarperCollins, 1992.

Index
▼